T0295838

Business Negotiations and the Law

Business Negotiations and the Law: The Protection of Weak Professional Parties in Standard Form Contracting aims to explore the issues surrounding contract negotiations between entrepreneurs and other professionals when one of the parties does not have the same level of bargaining power as the other. The need to protect weaker parties from unfair contract terms exists not only in relationships between businesses and consumers, but in business to business contracts also.

This book focuses on the problem of small enterprises, independent contractors and other professional weak parties and examines these from a European point of view. There are significant differences between Member States as to decisions regarding regulatory context on the protection of weaker professional parties in asymmetrical contractual situations. However, European businesses are overwhelmingly smaller in size, so protecting weaker parties becomes key in facilitating successful and efficient negotiations. The book provides a critical and comparative overview of the area and recent regulatory developments, both to clarify the direction that European legislation is heading, and to explore the tools needed to assure the effectiveness of the common market.

This text will be of interest to policy makers, researchers of European legislation, and students of commercial and business law.

Carlotta Rinaldo is a Researcher of Commercial Law at the Università degli Studi di Padova, Italy.

Young Feltrinelli Prize in the Moral Sciences

Roberto Antonelli, *President, Class of Moral Sciences, Accademia Nazionale dei Lincei.*
Alberto Quadrio Curzio, *President Emeritus, Accademia Nazionale dei Lincei.*
Alessandro Roncaglia, *Joint Academic Administrator, Accademia Nazionale dei Lincei.*

The Accademia Nazionale dei Lincei, founded in 1603, is one of the oldest academies in the world. Since 2018 it has assigned four "Young Antonio Feltrinelli Prizes" every two years, directed to Italian researchers in the fields of moral sciences and humanities who are less than 40 years old. Each winner is then requested to write a book-length essay on their research and/or the perspectives of research in their field, directed to the general public. The Routledge *Young Feltrinelli Prize in the Moral Sciences* series thus includes high-quality essays by top young researchers, providing thoroughly readable contributions to different research fields. With this initiative, Accademia dei Lincei not only gives a remarkable grant to the winners of the prize in order to support their research activity, but also contributes to the international diffusion of the research of eminent young Italian scholars.

Business Negotiations and the Law
The Protection of Weak Professional Parties in Standard
Form Contracting
Carlotta Rinaldo

Business Negotiations and the Law

The Protection of Weak Professional Parties in Standard Form Contracting

Carlotta Rinaldo

Routledge
Taylor & Francis Group

LONDON AND NEW YORK

First published 2020
by Routledge
2 Park Square, Milton Park, Abingdon, Oxon OX14 4RN

and by Routledge
52 Vanderbilt Avenue, New York, NY 10017

Routledge is an imprint of the Taylor & Francis Group, an informa business

© 2020 Carlotta Rinaldo

British Library Cataloguing-in-Publication Data
A catalogue record for this book is available from the British Library

Library of Congress Cataloging-in-Publication Data
Names: Rinaldo, Carlotta, author.
Title: Business negotiations and the law: the protection of weak
professional parties in standard form contracting / Carlotta Rinaldo.
Description: New York: Routledge, 2020. |
Series: Young feltrinelli prize in the moral sciences |
Includes bibliographical references and index.
Identifiers: LCCN 2019047237 (print) | LCCN 2019047238 (ebook) |
Subjects: LCSH: Commercial law—Europe. |
Business enterprises—Law and legislation—Europe. |
Negotiation in business—Europe. | Contracts—Europe.
Classification: LCC KJC2045 .R56 2020 (print) |
LCC KJC2045 (ebook) | DDC 346.407—dc23
LC record available at https://lccn.loc.gov/2019047237
LC ebook record available at https://lccn.loc.gov/2019047238

ISBN: 978-0-367-42052-9 (hbk)
ISBN: 978-0-367-82304-7 (ebk)

Typeset in Times New Roman
by codeMantra

Contents

Introduction

How far can a free and liberal market go so as not to result in anarchy, where the pre-legal dominance of the strong over the weak is in force?[1] Might does not make right under the rule of law, but in business relations it is a common belief that where only professional parties are concerned all transactions must fall within the framework of the fundamental principle of free competition. Protecting one of the parties of business transactions would distort the market mechanisms.[2]

Freedom of competition requires that economic relations should not be subject to dirigiste measures by State intervention, because the protection granted to a certain category of contracting parties leads to unjustified imbalances in the market. Even without sharing the extreme view supported by the anarcho-capitalist theories,[3] a State regulation in business relations should only take place to guarantee an effective competition and avoid market failures that could be brought about by wild economic initiative, thus precluding distortions of competitive relations. Regulation only aims at restoring and correcting the functioning of the market mechanisms, it is not directed to governing the economy or impose industrial strategies in specific sectors. Provisions should only aim at preserving the contestability of the market and this does not mean protecting individual market actors from potential damages.

---

1 Plato, 'Protagoras or the Sophists', in *Plato in Twelve Volumes* (vol 3, Walter R.M. Lamb tr, Harvard University Press/William Heinemann Ltd 1967).
2 Ennio Russo, 'Imprenditore Debole, Imprenditore-Persona, Abuso di Dipendenza Economica, "Terzo Contratto"' (2009) Contratto e impresa 120, 124ff. On this topic see also Mathias Mogendorf, *Der strukturell unterlegene Unternehmer* (Mohr Siebeck 2016) 20ff.
3 See for all David D Friedman, 'Law as a Private Good' (1994) 10 Economics and Philosophy 319–327.

Not all business parties, however, work on a fair and level playing field. They are not always well informed nor are they always counselled before and when entering into commercial transactions. Indeed, as Flume points out,[4] the eternal dilemma of private autonomy is that it is constantly challenged by an unequal distribution of power. This is evident especially when one considers standard contract terms in business-to-business (in the following: b2b) relationships. In predisposed contracts that are expression of a private normative power,[5] conditions may be included that shift the risk to the adhering party for an impediment or other contingencies, which the stipulator could prevent, overcome, or take upon himself at a lower cost; it could also be that the stipulator's cost of insuring against the risk is lower than the other party's cost. Undeniably, anyone can be affected by the unfairness of a standard contract term imposed by the counter-party, even professionals in b2b relationships.[6] It cannot be overlooked that there is a tendency among the better organised and more cunning economic operators to transform their freedom of contract into a regulatory power that is not free of dangers for the economic system.[7]

What if a professional party does not have the same strength as the other? There may indeed be strong differences in the bargaining position of contractual parties. Accordingly, in certain contractual situations between businesses there may be similar qualities of asymmetry as in business-to-consumer (in the following b2c) relationships.

This can be the case, among others, in the relationship between a trader and a large retailer, between a manufacturer and a purchasing centre, between an independent and a general contractor, between farmers, processors, traders and large operators in the food supply chain. In a very early example, dating back to 1906, the German Imperial Court recognised the asymmetry of the power relations in

---

4 Werner Flume, *Allgemeiner Teil des Bürgerlichen Rechts*, 2, *Das Rechtsgeschäft* (4th ed, Springer 1992) 10ff.

5 See especially Florian Möslein, 'Private Macht als Forschungsgegenstand der Privatrechtswissenschaft', in Möslein (ed), *Private Macht* (Mohr Siebeck 2016) 5ff with further references.

6 Specifically on the topic see Ole Lando, 'Should Business Enterprises Benefit from Consumer Protection', in Günter Hager and Ingeborg Schwenzer (eds), *Festschrift für Peter Schlechtriem zum 70. Geburtstag* (Mohr Siebeck 2003) 578. Similarly, Hans Schulte-Nölke, '"No Market for Lemons": On the Reasons for a Judicial Unfairness Test for B2B Contracts' (2015) European Review of Private Law 195ff.

7 For a discussion on power and its relevance in private law see Möslein (Intro, n 5) 2ff.

the negotiations between a ship owner and the operator of the Kiel Canal and therefore it did not enforce a term of their contract.[8]

Certainly, even enterprises can be in a weak position vis-à-vis a supplier.[9] Just like consumers,[10] they might be exposed to standard terms of business laid down by the counterparty, which they can hardly change, having very little contracting power. They do not deal with each other at arm's length with equal positions. Moreover, they usually have no other option, given that standard contract terms tend to align, this implying that going to another supplier they will get similar terms.[11] It might even be the case between a lawyer and a client, such as a bank, an insurance company, or a big firm, especially when it is the lawyer's main client.

As opposed to consumers who are individually entering into contracts for their own private benefit, professional market actors are generally part of a broader work and production environment, so that the contracts they stipulate involve directly as well as indirectly different kinds of stakeholders. The interests tangled in business transactions are therefore naturally more complex than the ones usually implicated in consumer transactions. The latter, in fact, are one-shot transactions between isolated players,[12] whereas the former have an impact, for example, on the interest of the contractual party's suppliers along the distribution chain as well as those of workers, investors, and partners involved. The unfair terms imposed by a stronger counterparty will tend to have a proportionate knock-on effect on all these parties, affecting a lot more people than the party to the contract.

The case of the US automotive-supply industry is very insightful: it is a pyramid in 'tiers', where Original Equipment Manufacturers translate their economic strength into transactional advantages through

---

8 See RG decision of 8 January 1906, in RGZ 62 264.

9 On the economic inferiority of some enterprises compared to their bigger counterparties see Alexander Stöhr, *Kleine Unternehmen* (Mohr Siebeck 2019) 68f and 71ff.

10 On the similarities between small businesses and consumers see Stöhr (Intro, n 9) 427ff, who, however, argues against a generalised application of consumer protection rules to business parties.

11 The fact that competitors tend to use the same clauses was observed as soon as standardised mass contracts started to spread as a consequence of the development of large-scale enterprises and impersonal contracting: see, for example, Friedrich Kessler, 'Contracts of Adhesion – Some Thoughts about Freedom of Contract' (1943) 43 Columbia Law Review 632.

12 For a characterisation of 'one-shotters' as opposed to 'repeat players' see Marc Galanter, 'Why the 'Haves' Come Out Ahead: Speculations on the Limits of Legal Change' (1974) 9 Law and Society Review 97ff.

standard terms imposed on their tier-1 suppliers, who, in turn, offer the same terms to their own suppliers in tier-2 and so on.[13] Considering the enormous economic stakes involved in the automotive procurement transactions for the market, the consequences – even in terms of money left on the table – of unfair and possibly inefficient performance terms cannot be underestimated.

The European Union treaded very carefully in the area of the protection of professional parties and largely shied away from broad forms of intervention,[14] apparently sharing the liberal idea that a State should only intervene in order to avoid market failures and functional distortions. In fact, the Council Directive (EEC) 93/13 on unfair terms in consumer contracts[15] does not consider merchant contracts, so that there is no common European rule (and no consistent policy) protecting enterprises and other professional parties from potential abuses of economic freedom by their stronger counterparties.

Consumers' law can sometimes indirectly also protect business competitors and it does happen that in many European Member States claims about unfair terms in consumer contracts can also be brought by competitors if they can result in alterations and distortions of the market conditions.[16] As a result, the provisions also safeguard busi-

---

13 For a very insightful analysis of the 'contractual DNA' in the auto-manufacturing industries see Omri Ben-Shahar and James J White, 'Boilerplate and Economic Power in Auto-Manufacturing Contracts', in Omri Ben-Shahar (ed), *Boilerplate. The Foundation of Market Contracts* (Cambridge University Press 2007) 29–44.

14 Cf Hugh Beale, 'The Role for European Contract Law: Uniformity or Diversity', in Francisco de Elizade (ed), *Uniform Rules for European Contract Law?* (Hart 2018) 18ff and 31; Christian Twigg-Flesner, *Europeanisation of Contract Law* (2nd ed, Routledge 2013) 65–67; Giangabriele Agrifoglio, 'Abuso di dipendenza economica e l'asimmetria nei contratti d'impresa (B2b)' (2008) Contratto e impresa 1356f with further references.

15 Council Directive (EEC) 93/13 on unfair terms in consumer contracts [1993] OJ L 95/29. For a first introduction to this fundamental piece of European legislation see Hans-W Micklitz, 'Unfair Terms in Consumer Contracts', in Norbert Reich, Hans-W Micklitz, Peter Rott and Klaus Tonner (eds), *European Consumer Law* (2nd ed, Intersentia 2014) 125ff; Peter Rott, 'Unfair Contract Terms' in Christian Twigg-Flessner (ed), *Research Handbook on EU Consumer Law and Contract Law* (Edward Elgar 2016) 287–313, 289; Andrea Mario Azzaro and Pietro Sirena, 'Il giudizio di vessatorietà delle clausole', in Enrico Gabrielli and Enrico Minervini (eds), *I contratti dei consumatori*, I (UTET 2005) 43ff; Guido Alpa and Salvatore Patti (eds), *Le clausole vessatorie nei contratti con i consumatori* (Giuffré 1997) with further references.

16 For the Italian law system see, for example, art 37-*bis* of the Italian Consumer Code, inserted in 2012, that entrusts the Antitrust Authority (*Autorità Garante della Concorrenza e del Mercato*) with the competence to ascertain (acting on a

ness competitors, whether weak or not. These provisions, however, pursue a different goal. They are not concerned with the balance or the regulatory structure of individual contracts nor do they take into account whether the negotiation process was substantially and formally correct. On the contrary, they only consider the suitability of private regulations of interests to ensure an adequate competitive dynamic, so it all goes back to competition and potential market distortions.

Unjust contractual arrangements can of course be detrimental to the balance and efficiency of the overall economic system. The market would be incapable of functioning properly as an open and competitive market. Moreover, the opportunistic behaviour of operators creating dominant positions would reduce output and result in a general increase in prices, to the detriment of all.[17]

Indeed, in one of the very few cases where the European Court of Justice (in the following: ECJ) engaged in a discussion on power relations between professional parties (*Courage*),[18] the disparities between contractual parties came to light in the context of a violation of art 101 TFEU. Here, the fact that one party was 'on a markedly weaker position than the other, such as seriously to compromise or even to eliminate his freedom to negotiate the terms of a contract',[19] was taken into consideration as one of the elements national courts

---

complaint received or on its own initiative) the unfairness of standard contract terms in b2c relations and to fine the enterprises using such terms in their negotiations. In the German legal system see BGH decision of 31 May 2012 (2012) Monatsschrift für Deutsches Recht 982 and, in b2b relationships, LG Freiburg, decision of 31 March 2014, Az. 12 O 12/14, BeckRS 2014, 7101 as well as *Bundeskartellamt*, decisions of 20 December 2013 (B9-66/10); decision of 22 December 2015 (B9-121/13); decision of 6 February 2019 (B6-22/16). In the latter case, for example, the German *Bundeskartellamt* initiated abuse control proceedings against a social network accusing it of the abuse of its dominant position on the respective market through the drafting of unfair standard contract terms. It prohibited the data processing policy this company imposed on its users and its corresponding implementation pursuant to §§ 19 and 32 GWB and ordered the termination of this conduct. On this proceeding, see *Tätigkeitsbericht des BKartA* 2015/2016, BT-Drs. 18/12760, 99 as well as the decision (for a case summary in English translation see <www.bundeskartellamt.de/SharedDocs/Entscheidung/ EN/Fallberichte/Missbrauchsaufsicht/2019/B6-22-16.pdf?__blob=publication File&v=4> accessed 25 September 2019). This decision is still *sub judice*; see Beschluss OLG Düsseldorf of 26 August 2019, Az. VI-Kart 1/19.

17 On this topic see Maurizio Bianchini, *La contrattazione d'impresa tra autonomia contrattuale e libertà di iniziativa economica* (Part I, Giappichelli 2011) 302ff with further references.

18 ECJ Case 453/99, *Courage v Crehan* [2001] ECR I-06297.

19 ECJ Case 453/99, *Courage v Crehan* [2001] ECR I 06297, para 33.

should evaluate in order to grant relief to a party to a contract liable to restrict or distort competition. Similarly, the Supreme Court of the United States of America held that where a party to an anticompetitive agreement is in an economically weaker position, so that in practice the terms of the contract were imposed on her, she can sue the other contracting party for damages.[20] The economic and legal context in which the parties find themselves and, at the same time, the respective bargaining power are therefore to be taken into account in order to guarantee private antitrust enforcement.

However, to ensure an effective answer and a real protection from unfair contract terms also for professional actors on the market it does not seem enough to react only when observing macro-economic consequences deriving from the exploitation of one party over the over. Injustice should be relevant also on a smaller scale. It seems therefore important – and, accordingly, it will be dealt with in detail – to carefully consider if competition law provides sufficient instruments or if a specific legislative intervention could be appropriate or even necessary in this area.[21]

Even when starting from the basic assumptions of a liberal economy, some Member States felt the need to legislate on the topic addressing this question expressly. However, these specific forms of protection from unfair contract terms in b2b relations differ greatly. Some Member States protect entrepreneurs even in cases when parties have equal bargaining strength: either the general provision defining unfair contract terms does not only address consumer contracts but any contracting party,[22] or there is a general prohibition of unfair

---

20 Perma Life Mufflers Inc v International Parts Corp 392 U.S. 134 (1968).
21 On the relevance of competition law in the context under scrutiny and on its adequacy as sole answer to the problems posed see more in detail in Ch 2.2. 'The role of competition law'.
22 This is the case for Germany (§§ 305ff *Bürgerliches Gesetzbuch*, hereafter BGB will be analysed in more detail below in Ch 1.2. 'Fairness control in all b2b contracts: the German case'), Austria (§§ 864a and 879 (3) *Allgemeines Bürgerliches Gesetzbuch*, hereafter ABGB), Denmark (Section 36 of the Act on Contracts LBK n 781 af 16/8/1996, see below, page 50), Croatia (in its civil obligations act), and Hungary (Act V of 2013 on the Civil Code, Section 6:102). After the French contract law reform of 2016 (*Ordonnance* n 2016-131 du 10 février 2016), art 1171 *Code civil* now provides for all contracts that 'toute clause qui crée un déséquilibre significatif entre les droits et obligations des parties au contrat est réputée non écrite'. It therefore introduces a new form of control over the content of non-negotiated contracts with respect to clauses that create a significant imbalance between the rights and obligations of the parties, and does so with no limitation to consumer contracts. On the topic see European Commission, 'Study on all mandatory rules applicable to contractual obligations in contracts for sales of tangible goods sold at a distance and in

terms in b2b transactions.[23] Other member States, on the contrary, choose to identify specific situations and certain contractual relations deemed worthy of protection because of structural asymmetries in the bargaining powers of contracting parties, only then providing professional market actors a targeted protection from unfair contract terms in their relations with stronger counterparties.[24]

The latter solution emerges also in the British legislation. Even though the English common law traditionally takes a largely non-interventionist approach to b2b contracts (notwithstanding the tools provided by the Unfair Contract Terms Act 1977),[25] the British Government recently decided to outlaw the so-called 'ban on assignment' (or non-assignment of receivables) clauses, i.e. any term in a contract that 'prohibits or imposes a condition, or other restriction, on the assignment of a receivable arising under that contract or any

---

particular online', <https://ec.europa.eu/info/sites/info/files/14_ september_-_final _ report_study_on_all_national_mandatory_rules.pdf> accessed 20 November 2019.

23 In France current art L 442-1, I, 2° of the commercial code forbids in business contracts all terms creating a significant imbalance between rights and obligations of the parties. The provision, recently revised by art 2 Ordonnance n 2019-359 of 24 April 2019, reproduces the rule that previously was in art L 442-6, I, 2°. The new rules do not replicate the specific prohibitions of particular unfair terms that were contained in the former version of the provision, such as those allowing one party to

> 'refuse or return goods or unilaterally deduct from the amount of the invoice raised by the supplier penalties or discounts corresponding to non-compliance with a delivery date or non-compliance of the goods, when the debt is not certain, liquid and due, without the supplier being able to check the validity of the corresponding claim.'

These rules are sanctioned by the nullity of the contract with restitutions, damages, and a civil fine (see now specifically art L 442–3 and 4).

24 This is the case in Italy: for a detailed analysis and evaluation of this case see Ch 3. Furthermore, Spain seems to be going in this direction, as reported by Mª Natalia Mato Pacín, *Cláusulas abusivas y empresario adherente* (Agencia Estatal Boletín Oficial del Estado 2017) 90ff. On the Dutch provisions (art 6:231ff Burgerlijk Wetboek, hereafter BW and especially 6:233), that do not apply to 'big firms'; see below, page 40. In Finland (Section 1 Act on the Regulation of Contract Terms between Businesses 1062/1993) and in Sweden (Section 36.2 Contract Act 1915:218, Section 2 Act on Contract Terms between Businesses 1984:292), there are provisions protecting business parties having an inferior position in a contractual relation, regardless of their size; on these rules see more in detail page 50f.

25 On the topic see Hugh Beale 'Unfair Terms in Contracts: Proposals for Reform in the UK' (2004) 27 Journal of Consumer Policy 289f and especially 308ff with further references.

other contract between the same parties'.[26] This is the first case in which a new provision limits freedom in business contracts in respect of terms that are in common usage in English law and are fundamental to financing arrangements in commercial relations worldwide.[27] The ban, concerning contracts that are entered into by all parties for the purposes of a trade, business, or profession, does not apply if the individual to whom the receivable is owed is a large enterprise or a special purpose vehicle (see regulations 3 and 4, also containing specific exceptions).[28] Indeed, it becomes clear that the provisions aim at shielding small and medium-sized enterprises with little bargaining power. It implies a recognition of the typical imbalance between the parties to a contract containing such terms and the difficulties of weaker business parties who cannot use all of their customer debts to raise finance through invoice discounting when such clauses are imposed on them.[29]

This trend seems to have found an echo in recent European legislative texts that recognise the problem of the weak bargaining position of certain professional market actors, intervening directly with rules that protect their interests in negotiations and limit the counterparty's contractual freedom as regards certain contract terms. This is for example the case in the very recently adopted Directive (EU) 2019/633 on unfair trading practices in business-to-business relationships in the agricultural and food supply chain[30] or again the Regulation

---

26 Section 2(1) Business Contract Terms (Assignment of Receivables) Regulations 2018. On these provisions see Dorothy Livingston, 'Freedom of Contract - A Justified Override: The Business Contract Terms (Assignment of Receivables) Regulations 2018' (2019) 20 Business Law International 63ff, who also discusses the different draft Regulations issued on the topic from 2015 onwards.

27 Livingston (Intro, n 26) 65.

28 Excluded from the scope of the regulation are, for example, contracts for the supply of prescribed financial services, contracts concerning an interest on land, and contracts of hire or bailment of goods. More in detail Livingston (Intro, n 26) 67f.

29 For an empirical analysis of how ban on assignment clauses adversely affect access to finance for small businesses and more generally raise the cost of finance for SMEs, see Hugh Beale, Louise Gullifer and Sarah Paterson, 'Ban on Assignment Clauses: Views from the Coalface' (2015) 3 JIBFL 463ff; Beale, Gullifer and Paterson, 'A Case for Interfering with Freedom of Contract? An Empirically-Informed Study of Bans on Assignment' (2015). Oxford Legal Studies Research Paper No 56/2015, https://ssrn.com/abstract=2677321 with further references.

30 Directive (EU) 2019/633 of the European Parliament and of the Council on unfair trading practices in business-to-business relationships in the agricultural and food supply chain [2019] OJ L 111/59. This directive prohibits certain unfair trading practices in the food supply chain and restricts the ways in which

(EU) 2019/1150 promoting fairness and transparency for business users of online intermediation services.[31] These texts identify specific situations of information and market power asymmetries[32] and the potentially adverse effects of certain trading practices on the businesses involved. The new rules aim at restoring an effective competition and a fair position in the contracting stage by imposing limitations to permissible contracting.

When comparing such different approaches, many questions arise. Market regulation may cause a significant decline in the actual meaning of the parties' contractual freedom. Indeed, protecting professional parties in their negotiations entails a noticeable limitation of their liberty in drafting agreements. How and why is this invasion justified? Where are the limits to be set in order to find the right balance between guaranteeing the correct functioning of a competitive market while at the same time allowing market actors to run the business risks that are inherent in the nature of their activity?

General terms and conditions tend of course to be self-serving, but the proposing party does not necessarily write them with the specific aim to expropriate value and to profit from informational asymmetries in order to create a disadvantage for the parties they are presented to. Boilerplate are instruments for an efficient business organisation, and they have always been considered a fundamental tool in the professional's hands. They allow contract standardisation and stabilise the meaning of transactions, while at the same time permitting the calculation (and potentially the exclusion) of the risks deriving from these transactions, so that they appear to be linked to the economic activity of the entrepreneur offering them.

---

contracts are made, varied, or terminated, as well as the content of what is agreed between businesses in their contracts. It applies to b2b relations where parties have strong differences in bargaining power, using the relative size of the parties (in terms of their annual turnover) as a suitable approximation for identifying asymmetries.

31 Regulation (EU) 2019/1150 of the European Parliament and of the Council on promoting fairness and transparency for business users of online intermediation services [2019] OJ 2019 L 186/57. For a critical analysis of its proposal, see Christian Twigg-Flesner, 'The EU's Proposals for Regulating B2B Relationships on Online Platforms – Transparency, Fairness and Beyond' (2018) EuCML 222ff.

32 So explicitly Recital 1 of the Directive (EU) 2019/633 as well as Recital 2 of the Regulation (EU) 2019/1150 (see also page 1 of the Explanatory Memorandum to its proposal).

Moreover, one cannot underestimate the fact that when the counter-party is herself an entrepreneur or another professional, it belongs to the normal responsibility of a market actor to be cautious with boiler-plate forms that are offered to her. The unfavourable consequences of unbalanced contract terms can be considered as part of the ordinary entrepreneurial risk they run when professionally active, so that the legislator should avoid invasive forms of protection.[33] Especially when considering sophisticated market actors equipped with legal counsel (*quisque faber fortunae suae*), they should realise how each provision in the contract can have significant effect on the division of surplus and should therefore act accordingly.

It becomes clear that an overly strict solution tends to erase the par-ties' contractual freedom and at the same time reduces the margins of the counterparties' entrepreneurial risk. A decision has to be taken carefully, as we are touching the very core of doing business.

---

33 Similarly, Agrifoglio (Intro, n 14) 1348f.

1 Unfair contract terms in b2b relations

A wide protective approach

Invalidation of unfair terms in all business transactions

It has been argued that especially as regards the use of contract terms 'also the enterprise, big or small, may need protection against unfairness'.[1] Regulation should therefore not only intervene in business-to-consumer contracts but also in merchant-to-merchant transactions, protecting all parties from potentially unfair and self-serving contractual templates presented by one party to the other. According to this opinion, even standard-form terms in contracts between sophisticated parties in high-stakes transactions should be subject to a substantive State-regulation in order to guarantee the efficiency and the fairness of individual negotiations.

This is in fact the choice made by the German legislator: the rules included in §§ 305ff and especially § 307 'Bürgerliches Gesetzbuch' (the German Civil Code, commonly called BGB) apply with minor differences to contracts between entrepreneurs, as well as to consumer contracts, regardless of their size and even in cases when economic power is evenly distributed and parties have equal bargaining leverage (see § 310 BGB).[2] Similar are the rules, among others, of the Austrian ABGB and of the newly revised French civil code.[3] Moreover, looking at soft law instruments, art 4:110 (the former art 6:110) of the *Principles*

---

1 Lando (Intro, n 6) 578. This is also the opinion of Schulte-Nölke (Intro, n 6) 195ff.
2 For a first commentary on these provisions see Peter F Schlosser, '§ 310', in Michael Martinek (ed), *J von Staudingers Kommentar zum BGB, Buch 2* (Sellier - de Gruyter 2013) para 1ff; Jürgen Basedow, '§ 305', in Franz Jürgen Säcker, Roland Rixecker, Hartmut Oetker and Bettina Limperg (eds), *Münchener Kommentar zum BGB* (Beck 2019) para 1ff and especially 34ff; Wolfgang Wurmnest, '§ 307', ibid, para 1ff; Jürgen Basedow, '§ 310', ibid, para 2ff.
3 For specific references and for further examples in other European Member States see Intro, n 22.

of European Contract Law (the so-called PECL)[4] applies to unfair terms which have not been individually negotiated by consumers as well as by professionals, so that the provided rules on substantive and procedural fairness are to apply to any contract, entitling the disadvantaged party to have the clause set aside and modified. Even strong enterprises and businesspersons are protected.

Although big business enterprises could negotiate and get better conditions if only they read contract terms carefully, they do not do it in practice. They are only interested in the essential terms, such as the quality of the goods or services, the price, the time of delivery, etc. Reading and negotiating the terms of the numerous contracts a firm subscribes would be costly and time-consuming. It would cause transaction costs, which on average could ultimately end up being higher than the benefit deriving from a successful negotiation.[5] This information asymmetry creates moral hazard problems, so that the outcome is lower in terms of global welfare, automatically generating Pareto inefficiencies. The legislative intervention, therefore, intends to avoid this second-best outcome, where standard terms shift the risk upon the other party for a contingency that the stipulator could prevent, overcome, or take upon him at a lower cost.

The choice to protect all business parties in their standard contractual negotiations is a policy decision based on economic considerations stimulated by a renowned study on the interaction between uncertainty on the quality of goods or services in certain markets and the solutions proposed for these situations.[6] This solution implies the political decision to understand standard contract terms as

---

4 Ole Lando and Hugh Beale (eds), *Principles of European Contract Law*, Parts I and II combined and revised, Prepared by the Commission on European Contract Law (Kluwer Law International 2000), 266. Here see art 4:110 (ex art 6:110) PECL–
  '*Unfair terms which have not been individually negotiated.* (1) A party may avoid a term which has not been individually negotiated if, contrary to the requirements of good faith and fair dealing, it causes a significant imbalance in the parties' rights and obligations arising under the contract to the detriment of that party, taking into account the nature of the performance to be rendered under the contract, all the other terms of the contract and the circumstances at the time the contract was concluded. (2) This article does not apply to: (a) a term which defines the main subject matter of the contract, provided the term is in plain and intelligible language; or to (b) the adequacy in value of one party's obligations compared to the value of the obligations of the other party.'
5 For these considerations see Lando (Intro, n 6) 577f.
6 George A Akerlof, 'The Market for "Lemons": Quality Uncertainty and the Market Mechanism' (1970) 84 QJEconomics 488ff. So Schulte-Nölke (Intro, n 6) 199ff:

instruments of market regulation: the rules allowing a judicial inter-vention assessing the fairness of the terms are meant for the protec-tion and improvement of market conditions. In this view, regulation in this area is to be considered a 'state infrastructure' discharging the adhering businesses from the responsibility of reading, analysing, and negotiating the boilerplate presented to them.[7] It is meant to be nec-essary for the sake of the efficiency of business in general as well as of the markets themselves.

An analysis and a critical evaluation of this solution in practice, the way it was implemented in a European Member State, will enable to discuss it and test it with a better understanding of its actual and oper-ative implications. Considering the different legal systems that opted for this choice,[8] the German system seemed the preferable one because it often acted as a role model in Europe for developing rules in the area of standard contract terms. Indeed, it is widely known that the General Terms and Conditions Act of 1976 (commonly called AGBG, so here-after)[9] was key in shaping the European rules on unfair contract terms in consumer contracts[10] and then later art 4:110 PECL,[11] which in fact

---

'Judges who declare lemon-like terms invalid and refuse to enforce them contribute to driving them out of the market and help solving the lemon problem'.

7 Schulte-Nölke (Intro, n 6) 210ff. For an application of this approach in b2c rela-tions and an analysis of the jurisprudence of the ECJ see Michael Schiller, 'Ine-quality of Bargaining Power versus Market for Lemons: Legal Paradigm Change and the Court of Justice's Jurisprudence on Directive 93/13 on Unfair Contract Terms' (2008) 33 ELRev 336ff.

8 See above, Intro, n 22.

9 *Gesetz zur Regelung des Rechts der Allgemeinen Geschäftsbedingungen* of 9 Decem-ber 1976 (BGBl I 3317). On the genesis of this act see Horst-Diether Hensen, 'Zur Entstehung des AGB-Gesetzes' in Andreas Heldrich, Peter Schlechtriem and Eike Schmidt (eds), *Recht im Spannungsfeld von Theorie und Praxis* (Beck 1998) 335ff.

10 On this see Hans-W Micklitz, 'The Principles of European Contract Law and the Protection of the Weaker Party' (2004) 27 Journal of Consumer Policy 349f; Jules Stuyck, 'Do We Need "Consumer Protection" for Small Businesses at the EU Level?', in Kai Purnhagen and Peter Rott (eds), *Varieties of European Economic Law and Regulation* (Springer 2014) 363.

11 See Ch 1, n 4. So Lando (Intro, n 6) 577ff. Similarly, see arts 79ff and especially art 86 of the CESL (Commission, 'Proposal for Regulation of the European Parliament and the Council for a Common European Sales Law' COM(2011) 635 final – 2011/0284 (COD)). They foresaw – before the informal but definitive withdrawal of the proposal presented by the European Commission in late 2014 – a judicial unfair terms test similar to those mentioned in the text. They, too, were strongly influenced by the German example. However, according to its Art 7 (1) 'Chapeau' these rules applied only if at least one of the parties is a small or medium-sized enterprise, as defined in art 7(2), and Member States could decide to make the CESL provisions available in all b2b transactions. On the significant

provide a substantive fairness control over standard contract terms. In fact, the regulation of *allgemeine Geschäftsbedingungen* is generally considered 'a glorious chapter in German jurisprudence'.[12]

Fairness control in all b2b contracts: the German case

As previously mentioned, in Germany the BGB includes a comprehensive regulation of standard contract terms that provides a substantial control over all kinds of contracts, even those between merchants. These rules apply to all pre-formulated terms[13] which one party presents to the other and are meant to be used for more than one contract, as long as they have not been negotiated in detail (§ 305 BGB). This is the case, according to established case law,[14] when the offering party was seriously open for discussion on the content of the clause[15] and gave the counterparty the possibility to influence it for the safeguard of her own interests. Individually agreed terms take priority over standard business terms (§ 305b BGB).[16]

A first set of rules concerns requirements for incorporation (§ 305 (2) and (3) BGB and § 305a BGB for incorporation in special cases) imposing the user (*Verwender*) of standard terms to draw his counterparty's attention to the provisions applying to the contract, thus giving

---

differences for b2c and b2b contracts in the CESL rules on unfair contract terms see in detail Stuyck (Ch 1, n 10) 362–363.

12 'Ein Ruhmesblatt der deutschen Rechtsprechung', Ludwig Raiser, 'Vertragsfreiheit heute', (1958) Juristenzeitung 7.

13 On the *Vorformulierung* as key criterion for the application of this set of rules see for all Schlosser (Ch 1, n 2) para 21ff.

14 On the interpretation of the requirement of the individual agreement between the parties see specifically BGH decision of 3 April 1998 (1998) Neue Juristische Wochenschrift 2600, 2601; BGH decision of 3 November 1999 BGHZ 143, 103; BGH decision of 23 January 2003 BGHZ 153, 311, 321; BGH decision of 19 May 2005 (2005) Neue Juristische Wochenschrift 2543, 2544; BGH decision of 22 January 2012 (2013) Neue Juristische Wochenschrift 856. On the topic Tobias Miethaner, *AGB-Kontrolle versus Individualvereinbarung* (Mohr Siebeck 2010), as well as Tobias Miethaner, 'AGB oder Individualvereinbarung – die gesetzliche Schlüsselstelle "im Einzelnen ausgehandelt"' (2010) Neue Juristische Wochenschrift 3121ff.

15 The BGH indeed refers to the individual clause and not to the contract as a whole. So, among others, BGH decision of 20 March 2014 (2014) Neue Juristische Wochenschrift 1725ff. On this, critically, Georg Maier-Reimer, 'AGB-Recht im unternehmerischen Rechtsverkehr – Der BGH überdreht die Schraube' (2017) Neue Juristische Wochenschrift 2ff.

16 For an unofficial translated version of the BGB see <www.gesetze-im-internet.de/englisch_bgb/englisch_bgb.html#p0417> accessed 1 April 2019.

him the possibility of gaining knowledge of their content.[17] Moreover, unexpected terms – that is, provisions so unusual that the other party need not expect them – are not part of the contract and any doubt on the interpretation of terms is resolved against the user (§ 305c BGB).[18]

As regards the incorporation, there are minor differences between b2b and b2c contracts. Only in the latter case, there is a specific obligation to communicate the general terms applying to the contract if they are not physically part of the contractual document itself. Business counterparties, anyway, have the right to gain knowledge of them upon reasonable conditions. Taking account of common usage in certain trades and of practice in long-standing commercial relationships where the terms were already adopted in the past, in such cases there is no need for express reference by the party presenting them and they become part of the contract even without specific indication.[19]

These rules on procedural fairness are followed by a 'grey' and a 'black' list of unfair terms (respectively, §§ 308 and 309 BGB).[20] The first contains a list of terms that present a substantial risk that the clients will be unreasonably disadvantaged, so that their effectiveness is subject to judicial appraisal, considering all the elements of the specific case. The second list enumerates terms which are unenforceable *per se* when included in standard business terms in consideration of their harshness, such as price increases at short notice or exclusions of all liability for defective goods.[21]

The substantive fairness rules are completed by a closing provision, § 307 BGB, laying down a general test for all terms, even those not considered in the fore-mentioned §§ 308 and 309 BGB. Accordingly, 'provisions in standard business terms are ineffective if, contrary to the

---

17 For a more detailed description of these provisions' normative content see among others Basedow, '§ 305' (Ch 1, n 2) para 54ff and '§ 305a', ibid, para 1ff.

18 Eckart Gottschalk, 'Das Trasparenzgebot und Allgemeine Geschäftsbedingungen' (2006) 206 Archiv für die civilistische Praxis 555ff.

19 Moreover, see § 305a BGB for special incorporation rules for terms concerning the provision of certain public services.

20 On the importance of combining rules on procedural and substantive fairness, as well as of combining floating and fixed barriers (such as grey and black lists) in situations of structural asymmetry see Florian Möslein, 'Die Regulierung privater Macht', in Möslein (Intro, n 5) 568f with further references.

21 For an in-depth discussion on these provisions see Dagmar Coester-Waltjen, '§§ 308 and 309', in Michael Martinek (ed), *J von Staudingers Kommentar zum BGB, Buch 2* (Sellier - de Gruyter 2013) para 1ff; Wolfgang Wurmnest, '§§ 308 and 309', in Franz Jürgen Säcker, Roland Rixecker, Hartmut Oetker and Bettina Limperg (eds), *Münchener Kommentar zum BGB* (Beck 2019) para 1ff.

requirement of good faith, they unreasonably disadvantage the other party to the contract with the user'.[22] In this 'reasonableness test' the judge shall identify and weight the interests of the two parties. He shall consider the contract as a whole as well as its aims. Also the clarity and comprehensiveness of the term are to be taken into account. In case of doubt, § 307 (2) BGB introduces two rebuttable presumptions. An unreasonable disadvantage is assumed if a provision is not compatible with the directing image of that contract according to default rules based on equity considerations ('wesentliche Grundgedanken der gesetzlichen Regelung')[23] or if it limits essential rights or duties inherent in the nature of the contract, so that the achievement of the aim of the contract is endangered.[24]

The provision in § 307 BGB is particularly important if one considers that, according to § 310 BGB, the lists under §§ 308–309 BGB are directly applicable only to consumer contracts. This does not mean that terms identified as unfair in the 'grey' or in the 'black' list – and therefore ineffective in consumer contracts – are always effective in business contracts, because they are nevertheless subject to the fairness control under § 307 BGB and can accordingly be considered unfair in relation to the specific contract. Therefore, in merchant-to-merchant contracts it is left to the courts to decide on a case-by-case basis whether a specific term is unreasonable and therefore ineffective, whereas the law does not require a consideration of elements such as the economic or intellectual superiority of one party over the other or further signs of asymmetry in the negotiations.

This has had major consequences in business contracts, especially if one considers, first of all, the strictness of the case law in recognising a negotiation in detail of the terms,[25] and, second, the severability provision in § 306 BGB: under this paragraph even if one term in a contract is unenforceable, the others remain intact.[26] According to the first,

---

22 Literature on this fundamental provision is virtually unlimited; for a first introduction and further references see Michael Coester, '§ 307', in Michael Martinek (ed), *J von Staudingers Kommentar zum BGB, Buch 2* (Sellier - de Gruyter 2013) para 1ff.

23 On the importance of 'Bestimmungen mit Gerechtigkeitsgehalt' for the identification of the default rules that general contract terms have to comply with in order to avoid failing the provided unreasonableness test see Coester (Ch 1, n 22) para 229ff and especially 247ff.

24 Coester (Ch 1, n 22) para 261ff.

25 For references see Ch 1, n 14.

26 On this provision see Jürgen Basedow, '§ 306', in Franz Jürgen Säcker, Roland Rixecker, Hartmut Oetker and Bettina Limperg (eds), *Münchener Kommentar zum BGB* (Beck 2019) para 1ff.

a negotiation of only some of the terms in a standard form does not exempt all terms from the fairness control of § 307 BGB, even if they were read and taken into consideration by the parties who decided to discuss only a few.[27] Therefore, terms that were looked into but not explicitly dealt with in the dealings – for example because the parties were in agreement, though unexpressed, on their content, so no debate was needed or because they decided to concentrate their dealings on other aspects of the contract they considered more important – may *ex post* be considered unfair by a judge, and therefore ineffective. Moreover, according to § 306, notwithstanding the ineffectiveness of such terms and conditions, all other parts of the contract remain in place and have to be performed by the parties. This happens regardless of any consideration on the importance of the ineffective clauses for the predisposing party and their role in the contractual balance. Additionally, German courts tend to reject the argument that a lower price can compensate for an unfair term: they argue that risks should be allocated to customers in general, not to specific customers who happen to be the victims of the unfair term.[28]

The extent of the protection to be granted in business contracts was one of the most controversial issues debated during the preparation of the AGBG in 1976[29] and it was very much criticised even after the rules were inserted in the BGB with the *Schuldrechtsmodernisierung* of 2002.[30] This holds, in particular, in consideration of how these provisions have been applied by the courts. Certainly, through § 307 BGB the judiciary control over the standard contract terms in business contracts has been very broad and it has gone much beyond the sanctioning of grossly one-sided terms that alter the spirit of the bargained-for deal.[31]

---

27 Schlosser (Ch 1, n 2) para 36a citing further literature and case law.
28 BGH decision of 12 May 1980 BGHZ 77, 126, 131. This was recently confirmed in BGH decision of 25 October 2016 BGHZ 212, 329. See Wurmnest, '§ 307' (Ch 1, n 2) para 43f citing further literature and Schulte-Nölke (Intro, n 6) 214.
29 See 1. *Teilbericht*, 99ff. See Basedow, § 310 (Ch 1, n 2) para 3 and Schlosser (Ch 1, n 2) para 1 with further references.
30 Among others see Klaus P Berger, 'Abschied von der Privatautonomie im unternehmerischen Geschäftsverkehr?' (2006) Zeitschrift für Wirtschaftsrecht 2149; Maier-Reimer (Ch 1, n 15) 1ff; Stöhr (Intro, n 9) 496ff. In the German press, describing the political discussion on the topic see Joachim Jahn, 'Vertragsfreiheit soll wachsen', *Frankfurter Allgemeine Zeitung* (Frankfurt, 16 March 2010) <www.faz.net/aktuell/wirtschaft/recht-steuern/kritik-an-strenger-kontrolle-vertragsfreiheit-soll-wachsen-1952089.html> accessed 1 April 2019.
31 Such terms, in fact, could have been declared void even according to the provision of § 138 BGB, stating the invalidity of transactions contrary to public policy.

While delimiting the scope of application of the judicial control over standard contract terms, § 310 (1) BGB provides that in contracts with an entrepreneur, reasonable account must be taken of the practices and customs for those business dealings and this rule has played an important role in the evaluation of standard contract terms in case law. However, although the 'grey' and the 'black' lists of §§ 308 and 309 BGB do not apply beyond consumer contracts, the clauses listed here are still taken into considerable account by the judges in their evaluation of unfairness. These lists have had a very strong indicative effect on whether the relevant term leads to a disproportionate disadvantage, and this has made it much easier for the courts to evaluate the general terms and conditions in business relationships.[32]

Indeed, in case law there is in practice no substantial difference between b2c and b2b contracts as regards unfair contract terms,[33] although a *Differenzierungsgebot* was specifically asked for in the parliamentary debate on § 310 BGB, where the main concern was to guarantee professionals the flexibility they need in drafting their contracts, and to avoid an excessive limitation of the parties' freedom of contract.[34] In decision-making practice, the burden of proof is reversed in b2b as well as in b2c contracts. Moreover, the party presenting the pre-formulated terms has always to bring evidence to the fact that the terms were bargained in an environment of free choice with meaningful informed assent, as well as that they do not undermine the value that the counterparty could rationally expect from the contract. This use of the terms in the lists as clues for assessing the unfairness, however, seems to undermine the intentions of the legislator, who had foreseen a specific evaluation of the *Angemessenheit* of the terms, to be decided on a case-by-case basis.

---

32 Basedow, '§ 310' (Ch 1, n 2) para 7ff; Stöhr (Intro, n 9) 496ff.
33 With reference to the old regime (§§ 10 and 11 AGBG) see BGH decision of 8 March 1984 (1984) Neue Juristische Wochenschrift 1750ff; BGH decision of 12 January 1994 (1994) Neue Juristische Wochenschrift 1060ff; BGH decision of 18 April 2002 (2002) Neue Juristische Wochenschrift 2388ff; BGH decision of 3 February 2005 (2005) Wertpapiermitteilungen 1089ff. With reference to the new regime see among others BGH decision of 19 September 2007 (2007) Neue Juristische Wochenschrift 3774 ff; BGH decision of 22 November 2012 (2013) Neue Juristische Wochenschrift 856 ff; BGH decision of 22 November 2015 (2016) Neue Zeitschrift für Baurecht 213ff; BGH decision of 26 February 2016 (2016) Neue Juristische Zeitschrift 2173ff. On the topic see Berger (Ch 1, n 30) 2150ff; Maier-Reimer (Ch 1, n 15) 1ff.
34 For the Bundesrat see *Stellungnahme zum Entwurf eines Gesetzes zur Modernisierung des Schuldrechts* [2001], BT-Drucks. 14/6857 [2001], 17. For the Bundestag see BT-Drucks 14/6857 [2001] 54.

This adequacy control takes place whenever a term has not been negotiated in detail, which can only be assumed when the user of the term has actually been available to bargaining and has granted the counterparty the possibility to influence its content in order to protect its economic interests.[35] This is generally denied when terms are unilaterally predisposed, and the relation is asymmetrical.[36] Yet the control is not limited to these cases, and the rules do not require the existence of imbalances in the parties' bargaining power, so that the provisions apply even in situations where the parties were free in their choices of drafting an agreement and of entering into it.[37]

Regulating standard contract terms and the role of entrepreneurial risk

It has been pointed out that a discussion on how the law should react to unfair and unbalanced standard contract terms presupposes an understanding of the fairness principle and of its relevance in contract law.[38] Indeed, since it relates to different possible concepts of justice, it implies a political decision. However, an analysis cannot be limited to considering contract theory and it is not only an ideological inquiry on the best approach to choose when regulating unfair contract terms. Enterprises are involved on both sides of the contracts, and the development and effective use of standard contract terms is for the firms offering them a key instrument of enterprise organisation. Their perspective and their

35 For references see above Ch 1, n 14. For a critical discussion see Miethaner, *AGB-Kontrolle versus Individualvereinbarung* (Ch 1, n 14) 156ff and 211ff; Miethaner, 'AGB oder Individualvereinbarung' (Ch 1, n 14) 3121, 3127; Nils Jansen, 'Klauselkontrolle im europäischen Privatrecht' (2010) Zeitschrift für Europäisches Privatrecht 69, 93f.
36 Berger (Ch 1, n 30) 2152f.
37 Critical on this point: Klaus P Berger, 'Für eine Reform des AGB-Rechts im Unternehmerverkehr' (2010) Neue Juristische Wochenschrift 467ff; Tim Drygala, 'Die Reformdebatte zum AGB-Recht im Lichte des Vorschlags für ein einheitliches europäisches Kaufrecht' (2012) Juristenzeitung 985f; Eva-Maria Kieninger, 'AGB-Kontrolle von grenzüberschreitenden Geschäften im unternehmerischen Verkehr', in Peter Jung, Philipp Lamprecht, Katrin Blasek and Martin Schmidt-Kessel (eds), *Einheit und Vielheit im Unternehmensrecht. Festschrift für Uwe Blaurock zum 70. Geburtstag* (Mohr Siebeck 2013) 177, 187; Robert Koch, 'Das AGB-Recht im unternehmerischen Verkehr: Zu viel des Guten oder Bewegung in die richtige Richtung?' (2010) Betriebsberater 1811.
38 Thomas Wilhelmsson, 'Various Approaches to Unfair Terms and Their Background Philosophies' (2008) XIV Juridica International 51ff. He identifies four different conceptions of justice: procedural, commutative, distributive justice, and finally justice used to support other societal policies.

interests are essential in any discussion on the topic. Furthermore, when dealing with b2b contracts, the professional activity of the adhering party should be taken into due account. One should not forget that taking on an entrepreneurial risk is inherent in the very nature of any professional activity and that businesses are repeat players.[39]

The rules controlling non-negotiated contract terms do not have as their sole aims the protection of the adhering parties' interests or the efficiency of the market where they operate. Limiting the discussion to these objectives means forgetting the true meaning of standard contract terms for the enterprise, thus leaving out all the considerations that, on the contrary, any discussion on enterprise organisation should entail. General contract terms are not in themselves an instrument to create inequality in negotiations. This may happen as a consequence of certain pathological situations and of the abusive and indiscriminate use of power by the predisposing party. Protecting the adhering party was always a very important element in drafting the rules, on a national as well as on a European level, since this form of negotiation can especially hide perils and forms of abuse. However, it is not the only reason for regulation in this area.

From a legal as well as from an economical point of view, the characteristic element in the case in question is the general will of the predisposing party to draft efficiently and to use standard forms for multiple contractual relations with several parties. Standard contract terms have the purpose – from a purely economic point of view – of safeguarding the interests and the contractual position of their author. They allow him to select, control, and calculate the risks assumed under a contract, excluding those which might be too hard to evaluate and to insure. A main role in the matter in question (and therefore in the regulation) is played by the entrepreneur and by his general will to have specific uniform contractual conditions with his counterparties with the aim of reducing the costs of production and distribution. The standard terms are an expression of his freedom of contract and the means through which he exercises his economic initiative.[40]

---

39 On the distinction between one-shotters and repeat players see Galanter (Intro, n 12) 97ff.

40 On this topic see the ever timely considerations of Ludwig Raiser, *Das Recht der Allgemeinen Geschäftsbedingungen* (Hanseatische Verlagsanstalt 1935) 18ff, Kessler (Intro, n 11) 631ff and Anteo Genovese, *Le condizioni generali di contratto* (Cedam 1954) 153ff. This is the general starting assumption, for example, in Lucian A Bebchuk and Richard Posner, 'One-Sided Contracts in Competitive Consumer Markets', in Omri Ben-Shahar (Intro, n 13) 3ff (see especially page 10: 'Courts

Especially in a globalised economy, liberty of contract plays a key role in allowing the shaping of standard contract models. The economic world has responded to the need for uniformity in negotiations deriving from mass production and mass distribution by attributing to the unilateral will of the individual entrepreneur a regulatory power that was previously unknown. Therefore, any regulation on the topic implicitly recognises standard contract terms as the fundamental expression of the general will of the entrepreneur offering them. It then explicitly limits the possibility to impose them conferred on her by protecting her counterparties with varying degrees of intensity that depend on political decisions, also in consideration of the concrete elements for the different possible cases.

The choice made by the German courts in this matter does not seem to give sufficient consideration to this 'enterprise perspective'. Indeed, when general terms and conditions are conceived only as an instrument of market organisation, and regulation in this area is only a means for disburdening any party (regardless of her capabilities and characteristics) from reading and negotiating terms, the relevance of such terms for the organisation itself of the offering party and the market role of the adhering party is left out of the picture.

Against this backdrop, the idea that a judicial unfairness test should spare all adhering parties from reading and understanding standard contract terms, in fact tends to underestimate their meaning for the predisposing party, eventually even to forget it on the whole. It considers them primarily as instruments to ensure a minimum standard and to avoid possible market failures that the adhering parties' behaviour would cause (mainly, the absence of competition of terms).

But then, how can it be true that the conclusion of tailor-made contracts is facilitated and that market efficiency is enhanced? On the contrary, if there is no need for negotiation over standard contract terms because judges have *ex post* the power to intervene, deciding whether the clauses are unfair or not, regulatory interventions might have a stifling effect on innovation. It is more convenient for the adhering party not to engage in negotiations at all and to accept standard contract terms without reading them, even if she actually could read them and

---

would do well to take a hard line in enforcing the terms of one-sided consumer contracts in the absence of evidence of fraud'), even though their analysis focusses mainly on the reputational concerns of firms offering standard terms to their client. For a critical discussion of the conclusions reached by the authors see Todd D Rakoff, 'The Law and Sociology of Boilerplate' in Omri Ben-Shahar (Intro, n 13) 201ff.

influence the content of the contract.[41] When an event regulated in boilerplate takes place and the application of a term leads to undesirable results, the adhering party can always challenge the single term in court in order to avoid its enforceability.

Such an increase in possible opportunistic behaviour not only seems to hem development and improvement in the offer of standard contract terms. It might also create a moral hazard on the part of the adherent, entailing more litigation and less certainty in business relations, consequently undermining the very reason for drafting and offering standard contract terms. This does not seem to increase competitiveness and market efficiency at all. In the end, it may turn out to be detrimental to the businesses' sense of initiative: all bargaining tends to become irrelevant.[42]

In the case, for example, of aircraft ground handling, contracts are usually drafted using standard contract terms, so that there is a predisposing and an adhering party.[43] The parties to such contracts, however, are not disadvantaged one-shot players; they are airlines, airports, or handling agents: namely companies of great economic strength, duly advised, that are repeatedly contracting within their core business. It does not seem fair to allow the adhering party (eg the airline) to knowingly take advantage of protective legislative provisions that allow her to avoid reading and negotiating the standard terms of the contract even if the predisposing party (eg the handling company) would have been open for negotiations. It might happen that a strict liability clause, such as one excluding compensation for any damage to the aircraft in the handling operations except in case of malice – that would have been enforceable if it had been object of the negotiations between the parties – might be considered unfair by a judge called upon to consider the standard term's application when discussing a specific liability of the handling company for negligence.[44] If the

---

41 Beale (Intro, n 25) 311f.

42 Stuyck (Ch 1, n 10) 368–369.

43 The general contract terms relevant in this business sector are standardised at an international level (Standard Ground Handling Agreement, SGHA) drawn up by the International Air Transport Association (IATA).

44 See the Spanish cases decided by the Supreme court – STS 14 July 2005 [RJ\2005\9617] and by the territorial court of Madrid SSAP Madrid, 20 September 2002 [JUR\2003\23128] and 14 May 2004 [AC\2004\1720], as reported by Mato Pacín (Intro, n 24) 71 and 222f. In this case law the discussion was on damage to two aircrafts due to collision of a tractor and a trailer; damage to an aircraft due to the impact of a water tanker supplying the aircraft; damage to three aircrafts as a result of loading and unloading operations; damage to two aircraft as a result of the

airline company had not seized the opportunity she had to discuss the disclaimer with the handling company and change the terms she was offered, even if she had the chance, then she should not be able to challenge it afterwards. One should not forget that she probably obtained a lower price precisely because she had agreed to the unfavourable boilerplate. Indeed, this decision should fall within the range of the ordinary business risk run by the adhering party.

It is not only a question of 'freedom of contract versus contract fairness', because reducing the problem of unfair contract terms between business parties to a discussion on freedom of contract as opposed to substantive fairness entails an over-simplification. When talking about b2b contracts one should never forget that much more than just freedom of contract comes into question. Both parties are professionally active and the contracts they enter into are the self-determined means through which they run their business and exercise their freedom of trade and profit making, which – at least in some European continental systems[45] – is a constitutionally protected fundamental right. Certainly, 'freedom of contract must mean different things for different types of contracts':[46] where there are strong differences in the parties' bargaining power this fundamental principle must be shaped so that the disadvantaged party can be put in a position to obtain a fair deal as regards the general contract terms, but this should not be the case when parties of equal skill and market position are dealing with each other.[47]

When statutory and judicial interventions are allowed to shape how standard contract terms should look, they authoritatively decide which terms are bad for the parties and should therefore be invalidated. This means that legislators and judges indirectly impose a certain way of running business, going against the principle of self-determination. The line is drawn in advance for the assessment if the State through its courts should enforce specific contract terms. Implicitly, it is telling the parties what is good for them and, therefore, replacing individual

---

collision of a tractor and a trailer; damage to one aircraft as a result of the impact of a water tanker supplying the aircraft; damage to three aircrafts as a result of the loading and unloading operations. In all three cases the disclaimer clause was enforced against the aircraft company.

45 See, for example, art 41 *Costituzione italiana*, art 12 and 14 *deutsches Grundgesetz*, art 38 *Constitución Española*, art 4 *de la Déclaration des Droits de l'Homme et du Citoyen* of 1789 (on the persisting validity of this principle see especially Conseil Constitutionnel, decision of 16 January 1982, n 81–132 DC).

46 Kessler (Intro, n 11) 642.

47 So Kessler (Intro, n 11) 633.

preferences. This paternalistic approach may be acceptable when discussing consumer contracts. Instead, it needs a more solid justification when the professional activity of businesspeople and professionals is involved. The latter, in fact, tend to be repeat players and, by conducting a business, they inherently run an entrepreneurial risk which should not be annulled with protective measures.

One should not forget that in any legal system there are always ways through which judges can have a meaningful substantive control over any contract and refuse to enforce it when it is grossly unfair and there is a significant and inappropriate incongruity: these rules range from those prohibiting usury to unconscionability, from doctrines such as duress or undue influence, to the provisions on mistake, misrepresentation, or *laesio enormis* in anomalous circumstances and eventually a general good faith clause. Such provisions allow a judicial intervention protecting all business parties when they really need it. When facing a pathological contract, remedies are typically offered by general contract law and these provisions may already address the problems satisfactorily. A general protection from unfair terms like in the German model, covering also situations where there are no asymmetries and bargaining weaknesses, tends instead to eliminate in the area of standard contract terms all business risk for the adhering parties. It therefore ends up protecting also those who irresponsibly are unable or unwilling to take properly care of their economic interests.[48]

There is no simple answer to the *raison d'être* of a regulatory intervention.[49] At the same time, though, one should agree on the fact that motives for regulation in a certain area are to be weighted differently depending on the context in question. In b2b transactions freedom in doing one's business should be enhanced and not limited by State intervention. Being responsible for one's business choices – if they are free – belongs to the ordinary risk inherent in every professional activity.[50] An excessive protection can lead to exaggerated risk aversion and can in the end stifle competition. Indeed, 'acts of competition

---

48 See also Ton Hartlief, 'Freedom and Protection in Contemporary Contract Law' (2004) 27 Journal of Consumer Policy 265f with further references.
49 Wilhelmsson (Ch 1, n 38) 52–53; Schulte-Nölke (Intro, n 6) 202.
50 In the glory days of British Victorian free trade see Sir George Jessel MR in *Printing and Numerical Registering Company v Sampson* (1874–1875) LR 19 Eq 462 at 465:
    'if there is one thing which more than another public policy requires it is that men of full age and competent understanding shall have the utmost liberty of contracting, and that their contracts when entered into freely and voluntarily shall be held sacred and shall be enforced by courts of justice. Therefore, you

should not too easily be qualified as unfair because they are contrary to what is usual or because they harm the interests of other economic operators'.[51] In the business world, the aphorism *caveat emptor* should to some extent still be in force: one cannot prohibit every unfair conduct in b2b relations.

In conclusion, the German solution, especially the way it has been applied by the courts, seems to have gone too far.[52] If entrepreneurs remain on a fair and level playing field, they should be free to define their standard contract terms.[53] It does not seem necessary to provide even big firms with such an invasive protection from general contract terms, as their situation differs greatly from that of consumers and

---

have this paramount public policy to consider – that you are not lightly to interfere with this freedom of contract.'
See also *Photo Production v Securicor* [1980] AC 827.

51 Stuyck (Ch 1, n 10) 369.

52 Many German scholars have been advocating for limitations and changes in the rules of the BGB; see, among others, Karlheinz Lenkaitis and Stephan Löwisch, 'Zur Inhaltskontrolle von AGB im unternehmerischen Geschäftsverkehr' (2009) Zeitschrift für Wirtschaftsrecht 441ff; Christian Kessel and Andreas Stomps, 'Haftungsklauseln im Geschäftsverkehr zwischen Unternehmern' (2009) Betriebsberater 2666ff; Felix Becker, 'Die Reichweite der AGB-Inhaltskontrolle im unternehmerischen Geschäftsverkehr aus teleologischer Sicht' (2010) Juristenzeitung 1098ff; Berger (Ch 1, n 37) 465ff; Menderes Güners and Tobias Ackermann, 'Die Indizwirkung der §§ 308 und 309 BGB im unternehmerischen Geschäftsverkehr' (2010) Zeitschrift für das gesamte Schuldrecht 400ff; Koch (Ch 1, n 37) 1819ff; Lars Leuschner, 'AGB-Kontrolle im unternehmerischen Verkehr' (2010) Juristenzeitung 875ff; Lars Leuschner, 'Reformvorschläge für die AGB-Kontrolle im unternehmerischen Rechtsverkehr' (2015) Zeitschrift für Wirtschaftsrecht 2045ff; Andreas Kollmann, 'AGB: Nicht nur theoretische Probleme (in) der Praxis' (2011) Neue Juristische Online-Zeitschrift 625ff; Drygala (Ch 1, n 37) 983ff; Werner Müller and Alexander Schilling, 'AGB-Kontrolle im unternehmerischen Geschäftsverkehr' (2012) Betriebsberater 2319ff; Werner Müller, 'Die AGB-Kontrolle im unternehmerischen Geschäftsverkehr – Standortnachteil für das deutsche Recht' (2013) Betriebsberater 1355ff; Hartmut Oetker, 'AGB-Kontrolle im Zivil- und Arbeitsrecht' (2012), 212 Archiv für die civilistische Praxis 203ff. In favour of these rules, but advocating for a different application depending on the specific elements of the case: Basedow, § 310 (Ch 1, n 2) para 16ff; Friedrich Graf v Westphalen, '30 Jahre AGB-Recht – Eine Erfolgsbilanz' (2007) Zeitschrift für Wirtschaftsrecht 149ff; Friedrich Graf v Westphalen, 'AGB-rechtliche Schutzschranken im unternehmerischen Verkehr: Rückblick und Ausblick' (2011) Betriebsberater 195ff; Friedrich Graf v Westphalen, 'AGB-Kontrolle – Kein Standortnachteil' (2013) Betriebsberater 1357ff; Jürgen Niebling, 'AGB-Recht – Aktuelle Entwicklungen zu Einbeziehung, Inhaltskontrolle und Rechtsfolgen' (2014) Monatsschrift für Deutsches Recht 636, 638; Maier-Reimer (Ch 1, n 15) 1ff.

53 For this conclusion in a comparative perspective see Ingeborg Schwenzer and Claudio Marti Whitebread, 'International B2B Contracts – Freedom Unchained?' (2015) 4 Penn St J L & Int'l Aff 43ff.

small enterprises. Business parties should be responsible for their own choices, when they were free.

Undeniably, there is less reason to protect strong parties from inequitable consequences. If they decide to spare the costs of reading the standard contract terms and do not negotiate clauses, even if they have the chance and the power to do it, then they do not deserve protection. Such rules seem to make it unjustly difficult for stipulators to use and enforce standard terms.

Accordingly, it does not come as a surprise that many enterprises contracted away from the very protective German provisions: by moving their seat to Switzerland and applying Swiss law, that foresees no such invasive control over general contract terms, they escape the application of the German rules in their b2b relations.[54] If only one considers the transaction costs enterprises chose to endure in these displacements, it does not seem a very efficient solution in practice.

Procedural fairness for all businesses

There are different ways for tackling the problem of standard contract terms. Indeed, excluding a specific substantive fairness test in business relations where parties have equal bargaining power does not necessarily entail that in these situations there should be no protection for the adhering party.

As already mentioned, standard clauses that are grossly unfair can always be challenged before judges according to the general rules of contract law, so that contracts agreed upon with fraud or force, without the basic guarantees of free will and consent of both parties, contrary to public policy or grossly in contrast with good faith and fair dealing can be invalidated in different ways and with different tools in any legal system. What is argued here is that where parties of equal strength are concerned a system that provides for a substantive unfairness control can stifle competition by introducing unnecessary rules

---

54 Berger (Ch 1, n 30) 2149; Klaus P Berger, 'Schiedsgerichtsbarkeit und AGB-Recht', in Hans Schulte-Nölke, F Christian Genzow and Barbara Grunewald (eds), *Zwischen Vertragsfreiheit und Verbraucherschutz. Festschrift für Friedrich Graf von Westphalen* (Schmidt 2010) 14; Jörg Kondring, 'Flucht vor dem deutschen AGB-Recht bei Inlandsverträgen' (2010) Recht der Internationalen Wirtschaft 184ff; Thomas Pfeiffer, 'Flucht ins schweizerische Recht? Zu den AGB-rechtlichen Folgen der Wahl schweizerischen Rechts' ibid 555ff; Thomas Pfeiffer, 'Die Abwahl des deutschen AGB-Rechts in Inlandsfällen bei Vereinbarung eines Schiedsverfahrens' (2012) Neue Juristische Wochenschrift 1169ff.

that inhibit business activities and entrepreneurial initiative. Such a logic of hetero-directional organisation is detrimental and does not seem necessary in an environment of free choice, because other and less invasive instruments can come into play.

Even strong parties are in fact in a situational disadvantage due to the pre-formulation and it is important to guarantee the authenticity of contractual consent. Therefore, even if no specific rule on commutative justice is necessary when discussing standard contract terms, it seems important to have rules safeguarding the actual consent of the adhering party, even when she is negotiating on an equal playing field. In particular, forms of procedural justice should be taken into consideration.

According to a by now long-standing legal tradition, legal systems usually have specific rules on transparency and incorporation as well as on the interpretation of standard contract terms that are applicable to all contracts, regardless of the standing of the contracting parties: terms and conditions have to be drafted in clear, intelligible, plain language and they have to be easily available to the adhering party. This is true, for example, for Italy in arts 1341, 1342, and 1370 *codice civile* (hereafter cc).[55]

According to these provisions – that apply to standard contracts where the adhering party was only offered the choice to accept them or not, without being able to influence the substance of the terms[56] – the pre-formulated contract terms drafted by one party are binding only if, at the time when the parties entered into the contract, the counterparty knew them or should have known them with due diligence (art 1341 *comma* 1). Moreover, certain terms that are particularly advantageous for the predisposing party or place special burdens or costs on the other have to be specifically agreed to in writing. These are the unfair terms (*clausole vessatorie*) exhaustively listed[57] in art 1341 *comma* 2: limitations of liability, clauses that give one party the power to terminate the contract or to interrupt the performance, forfeitures and deadlines, restrictions to the possibility of counterclaiming,

---

55 For a first analysis of these provisions see Alessio Zaccaria, 'art 1341', 'art 1342', and 'art 1370', in Giorgio Cian and Alberto Trabucchi (eds), *Commentario breve al codice civile* (Wolters Kluwer/Cedam 2018) 1437ff and 1483 with further references.
56 See more in detail Renato Scognamiglio, 'Dei contratti in generale', in Antonio Scialoja and Giuseppe Branca (eds), *Commentario del codice civile* (Zanichelli 1992) 262ff.
57 It Cass civ no 12044/2014; It Cass civ no 15591/2007, It Cass civ no 6314/2006; It Cass civ no 20744/2004.

restrictions to the freedom of contracting with others, tacit prolonga-
tion or renewal of the contract, arbitration or choice of forum clauses.
Furthermore, according to art 1342 cc, whenever a party predisposes
pre-printed forms and uses them to enter into standardised contracts,
the terms that are added prevail upon those stated in the form if they
are inconsistent, even if the latter have not been erased. Finally, if
terms are unclear, the interpretation should in doubt favour the adhering party rather than the predisposing one (the burden of *clare loqui*
contained in art 1370 cc).

Similarly, in Germany the §§ 305ff BGB provide, as already
mentioned,[58] incorporation rules that oblige the predisposing party
to give her counterparty the possibility of reading and understanding the terms as well as interpretation rules. Even if there are some
marginal differences in business and consumer contracts, so that the
latter have a wider protection in the negotiation procedures, even adhering business parties have the right to be put in a condition to know
which rules will govern their contractual relation and can benefit from
a favourable interpretation.

Likewise, Spain,[59] Austria,[60] and the Netherlands[61] have similar
rules on incorporation, transparency, and *interpretatio contra profer-
entem* that apply to any adhering party, whatever her professional
or non-professional standing. Also the Regulation (EU) 2019/1150
promoting fairness and transparency in b2b relationships on online
platforms includes a provision on procedural fairness imposing that
providers of online intermediation services shall ensure that their
standard contract terms are 'drafted in plain and intelligible language' as well as 'easily available' throughout the commercial relationship.[62] All these examples underscore the fact that procedural

---

58 See more in detail page 14f.
59 Arts 5ff *Ley de Condiciones Generales de la Contratación* (*Ley* 7/1998). For an
    insightful analysis of these provisions see Mato Pacín (Intro, n 24) 66ff.
60 § 864a ABGB, according to which unusual standard terms shall not become
    part of the contract if they are detrimental to the adherent party and if she was
    surprised by them, also in consideration of the circumstances of the case, un-
    less there was a specific reference by the predisposing party. For a discussion on
    this provision see Peter Rummel, '§ 864a' in Peter Rummel and Lukas Meinhard
    (eds), *ABGB Kommentar zum Allgemeinen bürgerlichen Gesetzbuch* (Manz 2015)
    1294ff.
61 In particular arts 6:231ff of the Dutch civil code (*Burgerlijk Wetboek*, hereafter
    BW). For an unofficial translated version of the BW see <http://dutchcivillaw.com/
    civilcodegeneral.htm>.
62 Cf art 3 of the Regulation (see Intro, n 31).

fairness is key to all rules regulating predisposed standard contract terms, even (one might say especially) in business relations.

Indeed, only business parties contracting on an equal playing field can actually benefit from transparency rules and from the rules on incorporation discussed above. In their case only can one speak of actual consent in relation to standard contract terms because, if the rules on procedural justice are complied with, they are in a position to read, understand, and negotiate the terms their counterparties offer them. It might also happen that there is a 'battle of the forms'.[63] This does not entail that standard terms are debated even though negotiations take place, so that they might not be exempt from substantive scrutiny such as the one under § 307 BGB in German law. Parties on an equal position can (and will, if this burden is not lifted from them) read, negotiate, and intervene on the content of the terms. Only their behaviour can really facilitate tailor-made contracts and avoid market failures. Only through real negotiation on terms, conducted by those who have the power to, can market efficiency actually increase. Freeing the market actors who could avoid market failures from their responsibilities does not seem the way to reach market efficiency.

However, as will be discussed more in detail in the next chapter, some professional parties do not work on an equal playing field with their contractual parties and their relations share the same qualities of asymmetry that one usually notices in b2c relations. Weak businesses, just like consumers, may be one-shot players and, in any case, they do not have the bargaining power to modify or set aside the standard contract terms they are offered and therefore in the contracts where they are involved a competition of terms will never take place. This deficit of contractual autonomy entails that the contents of the contracts they enter into might in fact be imposed on them. Even if they could understand the predisposed terms and dialogue with the proposing party, they would not have the bargaining power to effectively intervene on what they are presented with.

Even authors advocating for a substantive fairness protection of all businessmen eventually agree on the fact that not all professional parties should be protected in the same way. They ultimately recognise that clauses that should be considered unfair when imposed upon a consumer or a small professional may well be fair or even customary

---

63 On this phenomenon, see, among others, Giesela Rühl, 'The Battle of the Forms: Comparative and Economic Observations' (2003) 24 University of Pennsylvania Journal of International Economic Law 189ff with further references.

between business parties of equal strength, although they distribute risks unevenly.[64] In any trade clear and swift settlements are necessary, so that, for example, a clause excluding the possibility to offset reciprocally owed sums may not be unfair in b2b contracts. However, it might be considered as such if one party is in a weaker position and the clause was imposed on her against her interest.

Identifying which professionals deserve a substantive fairness protection from standard contract terms and the reason why this should be the case is not an easy task. Indeed, bargaining weakness in a negotiation is a relational concept and, as such, should be evaluated in relation to specific cases and circumstances where one can identify distinctive traits justifying a substantive protection like the one given to consumers. Even a big enterprise might be in a weak bargaining position if she is entering into a contract that falls outside of her usual professional activity, in a business sector where she has no experience. Having no knowledge of the typical clauses or of the uses of the branch, her situation is much the same as that of a small enterprise. This characteristic, however, and the difficulty in effectively drawing a distinguishing line do not exempt us from analysing the rationale and identifying general rules for this distinction in order to try and find a solution.

---

64 So explicitly Lando (Intro, n 6) 586, 597: 'a standard term which is unfair in a consumer contract may not be unfair in a contract between businessmen'.

2 Weak business parties

Weakness in negotiations and standard form contracting

It has been thoroughly discussed how the whole subject matter of standard contract terms is naturally linked to the economic activity of business parties and to the entrepreneur's subjective status. The modern organisation in the mass production and distribution of goods and services has led to extreme specialisation of companies. This, in its turn, allowed the establishment of large and influential specialised companies with a strong economic position. Relatively few companies detain a strong bargaining power and are therefore able to impose their standard contract conditions on their customers, who are rarely able to find other companies willing to provide what they need at better terms.

One could describe the problem arising from the abuse of this situation as submission of one of the parties in a negotiation and in a contractual relation through the imposition of unfair terms. It is well known that it is mostly addressed in relation to consumers. However, they are not the only ones who may find themselves in an asymmetrical bargaining position: differences can often be recognised in b2b contracts. Even small- and medium-sized enterprises (in the following: SMEs) and other professionals might be structurally weak and subservient to their stronger counterparties, for example because, being smaller, they cannot impose their decisions, or because – being economically dominant in another branch of production – they are negotiating outside of their core business.[1] Indeed, the protection of the

---

1 In 1987 the French *Cour de Cassation* decided that a business should be protected by consumer's law when negotiating outside of this professional competence, since they have 'le même état d'ignorance que n'importe quel autre consommateur' (Fr Cass civ I, 28 April 1987, D 1988, 1 note Delebecque), whereas this protection

weak adherent party in standard negotiations is of social importance also in b2b relations and should be pursued in a more consistent way: general terms and conditions are in fact able to influence and change substantive law in the way it is experienced every day by the community and produce unfair effects of far-reaching social scope.

Weakness is relational as it is bound to contractual relationships.[2] Moreover, information asymmetries are not linked to the production capacity of the parties, but rather to a variety of factors, sometimes connected to the complexity of goods and services offered, often in relation to the ability of one party to impose its conditions in the bargain. Business parties may not have legal counsel when entering into commercial transactions and may lack the tools and the sophistication to understand the contract terms that are offered to them. In areas where they are not repeat players, it might not make sense for them to invest time and effort to get better terms for their transactions. They might not be in a position to negotiate in order to better achieve their commercial goals or they might be entering into a one-shot negotiation. Even in contractual relationships between entrepreneurs there can be predominance of one party over the other with strong differences in information and market position, so that there are similar qualities of asymmetry as in b2c relationships.

A very insightful example in the area of merchant-to-merchant contractual template with a structurally uneven distribution of economic strength can be taken from the auto-manufacturing industry.[3] Here a persistent situational disadvantage of the suppliers does not only derive from the pre-formulation of the terms used in contracting, but also from the Original Equipment Manufacturers' market position. These strong differences in bargaining power are exploited to lay down self-serving terms that are not necessarily efficient for the system as a whole. This is especially problematic because such terms tend to build the 'contractual DNA' of the whole branch,[4] so that they end up influencing the terms offered by all parties working in this area. Other examples can be frequently found in the distribution chain: in

---

does not include contracts directly related to the business activity carried out by the party, where self-responsibility can be expected (Fr Cass civ I, 24 January 1995, D 1995, 327, note Paisant). On this topic see Martijn W Hesselink, 'SMEs in European Contract Law', in Katharina Boele-Woelki and Willem Grossheide (eds), *The Future of European Contract Law* (Wolters Kluwer 2007) 353.

2 See Micklitz *The Politics of Justice in European Private Law* (Cambridge University Press 2018) 324ff.

3 On this example see Ben-Shahar/White (Intro, n 13) 29ff.

4 So Ben-Shahar/White (Intro, n 13) 37.

this business sector entrepreneurs working in the lower part of the chain are often in a weak position in relation to their suppliers and terms tend to align.[5]

Furthermore, not all professional transactors are able, by virtue of experience and expertise, to recognise the various aspects of the transactions and some of them, just like consumers, do not have the same experience and expertise to draw on. An independent contractor, for example, is often in a weak position vis-à-vis the big enterprise. The stronger firm could force the counterparty to agree to unconscionable terms that would not have survived in an environment of free choice, for example limiting the ability to pursue a complaint or to seek reasonable redress and claim for compensation. Such clauses may alter considerably or even eviscerate the core deal terms that were negotiated and bargained. Big businesspeople, on the other hand, can afford to get advice if they do not understand a term and have better prospects of negotiating favourable conditions.[6] Furthermore, in case of a problem, it is more likely that a strong party can obtain an amicable solution, and she is not forced to abide by the unfair contract term.[7]

Asymmetries in contractual strength, moreover, are not limited to merchants' and enterprises' relations in a strict sense and might even be recognised in other professional activities. Even lawyers, accountants, or other self-employed professionals might be dependent on their main client (such as banks, insurance companies, big enterprises), so that they might be exposed to standard terms of business laid down by their counterparty. Having little or no bargaining power in relation to these strong clients, from whose employment they might even be economically dependable, they can hardly change the contractual conditions they are offered, even if they understand their hardship.

In such cases a strong party can damage the contractual equilibrium to her advantage creating inefficient and/or detrimental contracts. As far as experience and ability in commercial traffic are concerned, sometimes slight differences can be found between professionals and

---

5 It is well known that one of the problems in this context is the asymmetry in market power between businesses at different levels in the chain. As already mentioned (see page 9), this situation is now specifically addressed in Directive (EU) 2019/633; see especially Recital 1, 9, 14 and art 1. For an analysis of these 'hierarchical contractual networks' see Fabrizio Cafaggi, 'Contractual Networks and the Small Business Act: Towards European Principles' (2008) European Review of Contract Law 493ff.

6 See Galanter (Intro, n 12) 98ff.

7 Lando (Intro, n 6) 586ff.

consumers. Even the formers may not have the possibility to recognise (and consequently to protect themselves against) adverse effects that could result from standard contract terms. It may also be that an entrepreneur is aware of the general conditions of contract for the area in which he operates,[8] but the fact that he knows and understands their consequences does not also mean that he is able to object to their application. The stronger party might overreach and force the counterparty to accept unfair terms. Moreover, even if cases of structural weakness can be presumed, whether or not weakness is actually translated into economic disadvantages can only be evaluated on a case-by-case basis.

Already a very early and pivotal study on standard contract terms[9] – and precisely the first to identify the adverse effects of the absence of free choice due to standard forms on the correct functioning of contract formation – recognised that protection in this area needed to be granted systematically in all cases of structural asymmetry in contractual relationships.[10] Accordingly, it is now generally agreed that a significant imbalance between the contracting parties provides a deep legitimacy to limit the contractual freedom of predisposing parties by intervening into the standard contract terms with the aim of protecting the weaker party.[11]

Indeed, 'the constitutional right of freedom of contract is not simply a one-way street' and all parties should be equally free in exercising their influence in order to define the terms of the contracts they enter into.[12] This is not the case when economic and bargaining power is unevenly distributed. If one of the parties has such a position as to unilaterally define the terms of a contract, then it is up to the law to safeguard the fundamental rights of the parties involved in order to avoid that a contract, instead of being the result of the parties' autonomy, turns into a command of one party to the other: the concept of contractual freedom loses its meaning entirely when it turns into the dominance of one party over the other.[13] Therefore, in these cases,

---

8 Berger (Ch 1, n 30) 2151.

9 Raiser (Ch 1, n 40) 90ff.

10 Similarly, Kessler (Intro, n 11) 631ff; Genovese (Ch 1, n 40) 153ff.

11 Hans-W Micklitz (Ch 2, n 2) 331.

12 Schulte-Nölke (Intro, n 6) 203.

13 'Die Parteiautonomie verliert ihren Sinn – ebenso wie die materiellrechtliche Vertragsfreiheit –, wenn sie zur Herrschaft des Stärkeren über den Schwachen wird', Paul H Neuhaus, *Die Grundbegriffe des Internationalen Privatrechts* (Mohr Siebeck 1962) 172 and Flume (Intro, n 4) 10ff. This was expressly recognised, for example, by the German Constitutional Court, BVerfG decision of 26 July 2005, 1BvR 80/95

a state intervention is justified in order to find the right balance and allow both parties to use effectively and properly, if they want to, their freedom of contract.

The role of competition law

Against this backdrop, one cannot avoid considering if competition law can offer an adequate response to weak parties that are unfairly penalised in negotiations. In fact, these rules already provide for forms of protection that to a certain extent also aim at the defence of the weaker party from forms of private market power.[14] Reference goes to those provisions – common to all European Member States – on the abuse of dominant position (art 102 TFEU). Furthermore, given that the Council Regulation (EC) 2003/1[15] leaves the Member States free to decide on the opportunity to regulate power relations below the threshold of dominance, further national antitrust provisions may come into play.[16] Such provisions introduce forms of control over the content of contracts between business parties, eventually also pertaining contractual arrangements reached through the use of standard contract terms.

Starting from the ECJ decision *Courage*,[17] cases involving the exploitation of a weaker party by a stronger one through unfair contract terms have been posing questions relating to competition law.[18]

---

according to which a wholly *laissez-faire* approach – in the case in question, the German legislator did not provide specific rules imposing insurance companies to consider what the insured person has paid when determining her final profit participation – may actually turn into an infringement of the principle of contractual autonomy (*Privatautonomie*, art 2 para 1 *Grundgesetz*) and of the right to property (art 14 para 1 *Grundgesetz*).

14 On this see the fundamental work of Franz Böhm, 'Das Problem der privaten Macht: ein Beitrag zur Monopolfrage' (1927/1928) Die Justiz 324ff. For a discussion see Heike Schweitzer, 'Wettbewerbsrecht und das Problem privater Macht' in Möslein (Intro, n 5) 449ff.

15 Council Regulation (EC) 03/1 on the implementation of the rules on competition laid down in Articles 81 and 82 of the Treaty establishing the European Community [2003] OJ L 03/1.

16 See for example *Legge* 287/1990 in Italy (GU 13 October 1990, no 240), *Ley* 15/2007 de *Defensa de la Competencia* in Spain (BOE 4 July 2007 no 159), and *Gesetz gegen Wettbewerbsbeschränkungen* in the version published on 26 June 2013 (BGBl I 1750, 3245, hereafter GWB) in Deutschland.

17 See Intro, n 18.

18 In this case, the question deferred to the ECJ was whether a party to an agreement distorting the competition within the internal market in violation of art 101 TFUE (ex art 81 TEC) can claim for compensation of the damages caused by this agreement if it was imposed on her by her stronger counterparty.

Indeed, allocative efficiency, guiding competition law, and distributive justice, considered as the objective of the law regulating transactions between individuals, operate on different, yet overlapping levels.[19] Moreover, the bargaining strength of one party may derive from her dominant market position and the exploitation of the other may be a consequence of the abuse of this position. This imbalance, that is also relevant in the equilibrium of market forces, makes it possible for one party to impose her contractual will on the other, who accepts it without possibility of negotiation.

Although it is true that certain abusive situations such as the ones mentioned above may fall within the scope of application of the competition law rules, who might therefore be of some help for the weaker party, there are no reasons to believe that these alone can entirely replace a substantive fairness control over standard contract terms in b2b contracts.[20] In fact, the dominant parties' conducts that are relevant for competition law have to go beyond the specific contractual relationships[21] because the antitrust rules require, for their application, that the abusing conduct has a perceptible impact on the market and its structure. Competition has to be distorted, otherwise no protection is granted.[22]

In fact, it is common ground that competition law is not intended to remedy contractual imbalances but to ensure the correct functioning of the markets.[23] It focuses on aspects regarding asymmetric

---

19 Francesco Macario, 'L'abuso dell'autonomia negoziale nei contratti tra imprenditori', in Pietro Sirena (ed), *Il Diritto Europeo dei contratti d'impresa* (Giuffrè 2006) 292f shares the same view.

20 See Regulation (EU) 2019/1150 (especially page 2 of the Explanatory Memorandum to its proposal).

21 Mario Libertini, 'Posizione dominante individuale e posizione dominante collettiva' (2003) Rivista di diritto commerciale I 556f. On this see specifically It Cass civ no 22584/2015, and, more thoroughly, Trib Torino 11 March 2010 (2011) Giurisprudenza commerciale II 1471ff.

22 In art 102 TFEU it is specifically stated that any abuse of a dominant position is 'prohibited as incompatible with the internal market in so far as it may affect trade between Member States'. Evidently, if the behaviour affects only the national market and is not capable of impairing trade between the Member States, national law (for example art 3 *Legge* 287/1990 in Italy, art 2 *Ley* 15/2007 *de Defensa de la Competencia* in Spain, § 19 GWB in Deutschland) applies exclusively; see ECJ, Case 22/78, *Hugin* [1979] ECR 1869, para 17.

23 See for all Walter Frenz, *Handbook of EU Competition Law* (Springer 2016) 639: 'the primary purpose of the prohibition of abusive practices is, as it is the case with the prohibition of cartels, to maintain freedom of competition for individual undertakings and institutions as well as equality of opportunity and consumer well-being'.

negotiations merely in order to safeguard the competitive process in relation to the relevant market; it does not provide an answer for the main concerns related to asymmetrical power relations in standard negotiations. These rules do not deal with exploitative conducts apart from the cases specifically considered and they approach the question with a different perspective. Their main *raison d'être* is to protect public interests, not the weak party's private ones.

Nevertheless, it is not necessary to recognise a dominant position on the market or acts of unfair competition to see the exploitation of a structurally weak market participant. At the same time, an imbalance can be recognised in the very moment when one of the parties is able to impose her standard contract conditions on the other without giving her the chance to negotiate them. Abuses worthy of protection can be imperceptible on the market – from the point of view of competition law – due to the strong party's small market shares, while the existence of effective competition in a market does not have an impact on the reasons for introducing limits to permissible contracting when using standard contract terms. The cases that competition law can reach are therefore only a part of all the possible abuses that can occur in the context in question.

Even though competition law rules may *de facto* occasionally provide protection for the weaker party in standard b2b negotiations, conditions and purposes of these provisions are different from those of a regulation focused on protecting the adherent party on the ground of her weakness. The control that can be exercised over unfair terms by the means of competition law is much more limited than what can be achieved through forms of substantive fairness control over standard contract terms. Therefore, these mechanisms do not seem to suffice when weak business parties are concerned.

If one of the parties has not had the opportunity to take part in the definition of the content of the contract and this is imposed on her due to disparities in the negotiating power of parties, it cannot be said that the resulting contract is an expression of the freedom and equality of the contracting parties. No rules on competition can offer a comprehensive solution to this problem. Freedom of contract cannot be preserved by the existence of a competitive market and competition

---

See also Giuseppe Colangelo, *L'abuso di dipendenza economica tra disciplina della concorrenza e diritto dei contratti. Un'analisi economica e comparata* (Giappichelli 2004) 11ff. In a general perspective see Franz Böhm, 'Demokratie und ökonomische Macht' in Institut für Ausländisches und Internationales Wirtschaftsrecht (ed), *Kartelle und Monopole* (vol I, Müller 1961) 3ff; Böhm (Ch 2, n 14) 324ff.

law in its strict sense is not sufficient to ensure fair negotiations in b2b relations.[24]

If a distributive justice demands that weaker market participants should be defended at the expense of stronger ones – whether or not it affects the market and whether or not there is competition – then this explains and validates a judicial intervention into contracts where unfair terms were imposed to the adherent.

This conclusion is further reinforced if one considers, from a historical perspective, that in Germany, the country where the problem of standard contract terms was first addressed by the courts and the literature,[25] the control over the so-called *AGB* first developed out of competition law.[26] Indeed, if one reads the first relevant decisions of the Imperial Court and later of the Federal Court, two elements come to light: firstly, all cases concern b2b relations and, secondly, the courts' arguments are based on considerations regarding the power gap that is typical in standard contracting. Accordingly, the resulting judgements were based on the recognition of the dominant or monopoly market position of the party offering standard contract terms.[27] This way of dealing with the problem, however, was soon discarded in the subsequent case law as it could not guarantee a satisfactory answer for all cases worthy of protection. The courts recognised that it could still allow the enforceability of contracts and contract terms unilaterally dictated by one of the parties, imposing on the adherent an unreasonable risk or an unfair burden in cases where this abuse did not result in a dominant position in the market.[28]

Such considerations lead us to appreciate the fact that relying only on the provisions of competition law does not seem to solve effectively the problem we are faced with. A specific protection of the weaker professional seems therefore adequate, as acknowledged even by the

---

24 Stuyck (Ch 1, n 10) 366. Similarly, Mato Pacìn (Intro, n 24) 133ff.

25 See above, page 13 and especially Raiser (Ch 1, n 40).

26 On this see specifically Jürgen Basedow, 'Vorbemerkung vor § 305', in Franz Jürgen Säcker, Roland Rixecker, Hartmut Oetker and Bettina Limperg (eds), *Münchener Kommentar zum BGB* (Beck 2019) para 11–12 with further references.

27 See for example RG decision of 8 January 1906 RGZ 62, 264, 266; RG decision of 26 October 1921 RGZ 103, 82, 83; RG decision of 21 March 1923 RGZ 106, 386; BGH decision of 13 March 1956 (1956) Neue Juristiche Wochenschrift 1066.

28 Indeed, the courts acknowledged that such an unjust situation may occur notwithstanding the market position of the offering party, so explicitly BGH decision of 29 October 1962 (1963) Neue Juristiche Wochenschrift 99; BGH, decision of 17 February 1964 (1964) Neue Juristiche Wochenschrift 1123.

critics of the German choice.[29] In consideration of the very different answers that can be given to the question in this continuum of cases, it seems important to analyse if and under which conditions rules protecting adherent parties in their commercial transactions should be applied in b2b relationships. Nevertheless, it must be kept in mind that, in any case, businesspeople should be allowed to freely agree on the distribution of risk they prefer, if there is an individual negotiation. They should be responsible for their own choices, when they are free.

Defining weak business parties

In some respects, disparities in contractual power can even be considered congenital to the very nature of market transactions. Weakness, indeed, is a relational concept that should in principle be judged in relation to specific contracts. It cannot be defined a priori as a status because, even if structural weakness in certain situations can be presumed, only in the particular case can one assess if this position determined the imposition of standard terms without the possibility to influence them.[30] Delimiting the category of businesses worthy of protection in this area might therefore entail some uncertainties as to the scope and application of protective rules, and it could lead to unpredictability in business relations.

A way to elude such uncertainties could be to grant protection to business parties according to their size. In fact, small business parties tend to be more exposed to the counterparties' contractual abuses than bigger ones.[31] This way, unambiguously quantifiable criteria can be taken into account and they can be used to identify clear categories of protected parties. To this end, one can draw inspiration from the European regulations, where a definition of micro, small, and medium-sized enterprises can be found. In fact, the Commission Recommendation of 6 May 2003 distinguishes enterprises into different categories according

---

29 Berger (Ch 1, n 30) 2156:
'Wenn auf beiden Seiten eines Rechtsgeschäfts Unternehmer stehen, ist die kein Garant für das Funktionieren der Richtigkeitsgewähr des Vertragskonsenses. Die AGB-Kontrolle ist auch im unternehmerischen Geschäftsverkehr sinnvoll und geboten. Erforderlich ist aber eine Neukalibrierung der Eingriffs- und Kontrollschwelle für die AGB-rechtliche Inhaltskontrolle vor dem Hintergrund der im Gesetz angelegten Differenzierung zwischen b2c und b2b-Geschäft.'
See also Basedow (Ch 1, n 2) para 18.
30 Micklitz (Ch 2, n 2) 324.
31 On this topic see especially Stöhr (Intro, n 9) 56ff with further references.

to their size in consideration of precise empirical elements such as staff number, turnover, and balance sheet total.[32]

This approach was followed, with specific reference to the application of the rules on standard contract terms, in the Netherlands: here the legislator opted for a clearly quantifiable distinction between big and small enterprises. In the Dutch civil code, a general clause (art 6:233 BW) provides that a standard contract term may be set aside if it is unreasonably onerous for the adherent party and if the stipulator has not given the other party a reasonable opportunity to take cognisance of the general conditions according to the provisions of art 6:234 BW. These rules, even if they do not distinguish between professional and non-professional adherent parties, do not apply indiscriminately to all, because art 6:235(1) BW states that the aforementioned provisions cannot be invoked by legal persons obliged to publish their annual financial statements and by other enterprises in which more than 50 persons are employed.[33] Such businesses, thus excluded from the category of small enterprises, can only invoke the general clause in art 6:248(2) BW – applicable to all contracts and to all terms, even those that the parties negotiated individually – according to which a rule binding upon the parties under a contract does not apply to the extent that under the circumstances this would be unacceptable by the standards of reasonableness and equity.[34]

---

32 Commission recommendation of 6 May 2003 n 361 concerning the definition of micro, small, and medium-sized enterprises [2003] OJ L 124/36, Annex. Accordingly, enterprises are all entities engaged in an economic activity, irrespective of their legal forms. This includes, in particular, self-employed persons and family businesses engaged in craft or other activities, partnerships, or associations regularly engaged in an economic activity (art 1). In detail, according to art 2 (Staff headcount and financial ceilings determining enterprise categories):

'(1). The category of micro, small and medium-sized enterprises (SMEs) is made up of enterprises that employ fewer than 250 persons and which have an annual turnover not exceeding EUR 50 million, and/or an annual balance sheet total not exceeding EUR 43 million. (2). Within the SME category, a small enterprise is defined as an enterprise which employs fewer than 50 persons and whose annual turnover and/or annual balance sheet total does not exceed EUR 10 million. (3) Within the SME category, a micro enterprise is defined as an enterprise which employs fewer than 10 persons and whose annual turnover and/or annual balance sheet total does not exceed EUR 2 million.'

33 For an unofficial translated version of the BW see <http://dutchcivillaw.com/civil codegeneral.htm>.

34 Lando (Intro, n 6).

Size alone, however, does not necessarily imply information asymmetries, economic dependence, or unsophistication in business transactions. Any distinction based only on size is therefore to a large extent arbitrary. Moreover, it tends to create rather broad and heterogeneous categories, with already defined subcategories (such as medium-sized, small, and micro enterprises), where different kinds of businesses are included, ranging from self-employed professionals and family businesses to venture capital companies, from craft enterprises to high-tech companies.[35] In this respect, differences in terms of economic power between professionals belonging to the same category can be very significant.

A small-sized high-tech company with eg 48 employees is in fact hardly comparable, in terms of relative bargaining strength and experience, to a family micro-sized business engaged in craft activities. The imbalances in the relation between such professional parties, all falling within the category of SMEs, might be the same as between a medium-sized and a large company. This might not be problematic when the distinction is relevant for the purpose of identifying the beneficiaries of specific favourable policies or funding plans in the context of the Commission strategies, which is indeed the main objective of the Commission's official definition mentioned above. Things change when the purpose is to apply a different and protective contractual regime to a specific category of professionals.[36]

Therefore, it does not seem appropriate to rely only on quantitative criteria and sharp distinctions. In fact, they might turn out to be too rigid. They might lead to strategic behaviour and to disputes on the formal statutes of the parties rather than allowing a substantive evaluation of the underlying contractual relations. Even though they guarantee predictability, they are difficult to maintain and rarely turn out to be helpful.[37] The identification of situations that need to be protected should, in fact, also consider other elements that point at the existence of an asymmetry between the parties as concerns for their bargaining power.

With reference to the criteria for the assessment of weakness in negotiations, the Directive (EU) 2019/633 on unfair trading practices in

---

35 See, with specific reference to the category of SMEs according to the European Commission's definition, Hesselink (Ch 2, n 1) 350f. On the problem of small businesses see especially Larry Garvin, 'Small Businesses and the False Dichotomies of Contract Law' (2005) 40 Wake Forest Law Review 296f, who defines small business an 'assorted group', where generalisations are hazardous.

36 Hesselink (Ch 2, n 1) 351ff.

37 Micklitz (Ch 2, n 2) 321.

business-to-business relationships in the agricultural and food supply chain goes a step further. While still basing the distinction between protected and non-protected parties on clearly quantifiable elements, it relies on annual turnover considering it as a suitable approximation for relative bargaining power and as a symptom of asymmetry.[38] Moreover, it adopts a dynamic approach and recognises that size is not relevant in absolute values, but only in relation to the size of the counterparty. Accordingly, it does not only address SMEs: in defining the scope of application of the rules it provides, it distinguishes five categories of sale contracts in the agricultural and food supply chain that are identified by the fact that suppliers are smaller than their buyers – this being an indicator of bargaining weakness.

Other elements, however, should also be taken into account. As already observed, asymmetries can be structural and they characterise specific contractual relations, such as franchising, subcontracting agreements, agency.[39] Furthermore, information asymmetries or inferiority in market position can entail the subservience of one of the parties in a contractual relation.

This happens, for example, to professionals dealing outside of their core business: even though they are repeat players in their own field, they are one-shotters in relation to an occasional contract outside of it. When a leading firm for catering services deals with a high-tech company for the purchase of computer hardware, it does not do so in the same position as when she is negotiating with her food suppliers. In such a situation, she is unlikely to be in a position to obtain the terms she wants, and it is hardly reasonable for her to engage in lengthy and complicated negotiations when she only occasionally enters into contracts in a certain area of business. Moreover, an entrepreneur who could be easily substituted by the counterparty typically has less market strength than the irreplaceable counterparty, especially if specific investments were made for that contractual relation.

As suggested by the choice made in the Directive (EU) 2019/633, size and commercial strength should be taken into account as a presumptive element of weakness. They can be used as absolute values (especially when these values are either very big or very small), but they especially matter, as relative values, in the comparison between the sizes of the parties to a contract. A certain commercial strength, measured using objective criteria such as annual turnover and the

---

38 Recital 9, 14 and art 1 subs 2 of the Directive (EU) 2019/633.
39 Mogendorf (Intro, n 2) 10ff.

other elements mentioned in the European definition, can be used as a suitable approximation in order to assume that a large entrepreneur should be able to monitor and observe through her staff the market upon which she operates regularly, as well as engage legal counsel when entering into important transactions, thus overcoming information asymmetries in negotiations. On the contrary, this cannot be assumed for micro-sized businesses. But a middle-sized enterprise has no bargaining power in relation to a large entrepreneur with more commercial strength, so that the potential absence of information asymmetries would not be of much use.

Nevertheless, there are circumstances where specific situational disadvantages come into play, and here size is not the only element pointing to imbalances in bargaining power. This is for example the case in relationships between online intermediation service providers and business users. Accordingly, the regulation of 'unilaterally determined' terms and conditions in b2b relationships on online platforms[40] does not consider quantitative requirements for the application of the substantive protective rules, nor does it only apply to SMEs, even though the protection of these enterprises is the Commission's main concern.[41] It assumes that providers will have a set of standard contract terms, which will effectively be imposed on any business user seeking to use the online intermediation services.

Other criteria such as legal and trade experience could also ideally come into consideration.[42] However, such subjective criteria are difficult to define in a normative way and their adoption would lead to uncertainties in the identification of weak business parties. How can one assess if a person entering into a franchise contract as a franchisee does or does not have enough business experience to take care of his own interests? Why should it matter that the prospective contractual party took a law degree? These elements may not have any clear and definite additional value when assessing weakness in negotiations, so that they should not be regarded when defining who should obtain specific protection.

Leaving these and similar subjective circumstances aside, the objective conditions mentioned above enable an identification of those b2b

---

40 See art 2 Regulation (EU) 2019/1150. See above (Intro, n 31).
41 See already the Communication on Online Platforms and the Digital Single Market – opportunities and Challenges for Europe ('Platform Communication') COM (2016) 288 final.
42 On this Mogendorf (Intro, n 2) 12f.

cases in which the contractual freedom of one of the parties cannot be properly exercised. This translates into the possibility for the other to overreach and impose unreasonably one-sided contractual conditions. The content of a contract stipulated under these conditions corresponds therefore only formally, but not substantively, to the will of both parties,[43] albeit the mutual assent, because the weak party is faced with the choice of whether to accept the proposed contract or not to enter into it. Such a strong limitation of contractual autonomy entails in fact a need of protection that justifies a regulatory intervention.

Objectives and rationales for the protection of the weak business parties

One could of course argue that in all the cases mentioned above, notwithstanding the situational disadvantages, there is a lower need of protection for businesses in comparison to consumers, because freedom of contract should be regarded as a cornerstone in the market economy and professional actors have to consider the risks they are taking in the course of their activity.[44] No one is obliged to carry out a business and access to trade is free and never necessary. One could therefore claim that those who do it voluntarily should bear the risks inherent in commerce, so that they should fall beyond the sphere of protection expressly ensured by the legislator. This area, one may argue, should be limited only to the fundamental sectors relating to necessary goods and elementary necessities of life:[45] the law should for example monitor the work-related conditions and the relation between salaried employees and employers; it should protect tenants versus landlords, the insured versus the insurer, the consumer versus the professional.[46] Apart from these areas, contract law should only facilitate the efforts of contracting parties to independently maximise

---

43 More in detail, for a discussion on the difference between formal freedom and substantial justice, see among others Möslein (Intro, n 5) 5ff; Christian Heinrich, *Formale Freiheit und materiale Gerechtigkeit* (Mohr Siebeck 2000); Dieter Reuter, 'Die etischen Grundlagen des Privatrechts – formale Freiheitsethik oder materiale Verantwortungsethik?' (1989) 189 Archiv für die civilistische Praxis 199ff.

44 For this view, see for example, Richard Calnan, 'Ban the Ban: Prohibiting Restrictions on the Assignment of Receivables' (2018) 5 JIBFL 136–137. For an analysis of these considerations see Mogendorf (Intro, n 2) 20ff.

45 Hartlief (Ch 1, n 48) 255.

46 On the importance of protecting these groups see in a general perspective Eike von Hippel, *Der Schutz des Schwächeren* (Mohr Siebeck 1982) 1ff.

the joint gains from transactions. The business enterprise, whatever its size, should take care of itself, and needs no protection. It faces stipulators that are business partners and should be ready to read the counterparty's general conditions. Furthermore, a professional should be less optimistic than a consumer as regards the contingencies and risks dealt with in the standard form contracts.

This position is not generally shared by scholars. Even those who advocate for an ample freedom of contract for firms and aim at making contract law a merchants' law without redistributive or fair legal rules that do not maximise joint surplus[47] only apply their theories to 'sophisticated parties', explicitly excluding small enterprises and independent contractors from their analysis.[48] The stronger party may have abused of his power by taking advantage of the other party's weakness, and this may suffice to set aside or modify the contract.[49] A small enterprise may have the same difficulties as a consumer in understanding the terms of the stipulator's general conditions. He might also be in a state of dependence on the stipulator (he owes money, or he is the main customer) that forces him to accept unfair terms.

Evidently, the choice to protect the weak professional from the general terms of contract imposed by the counterparty is a policy decision which can be freely scaled in its breadth and intensity. It is not necessary to intervene in all cases, but there are many reasons that lead in the direction of regulation.

A legislator should in fact consider distributional goals as well as contractual fairness, and of course a competitive market depends heavily on an effective freedom of contract, which cannot be limited to a mere and unsubstantial assertion. When an entrepreneur is structurally dependent on his counterparty and there is asymmetrical information, strong firms are tempted to overreach and there can hardly be a healthy competition. As for standard contract conditions, one can assume that conditions which unjustly benefit the strong party at the expense of the weak one will come to prevail, instead of those that would be better in terms of economic efficiency.

A limitation of permissible contracting to protect the weak confines the possibility for the strong party to impose unpredictable and not apparent (therefore not justified) costs on the counterparty. It allows the unsophisticated entrepreneur to only analyse and compare the

---

47 See for example Alan Schwartz and Robert Scott, 'Contracts theory and the limits of contract law' (2003) 113 YaleLJ 541ff.

48 Schwartz and Scott (Ch 2, n 47) 545ff.

49 Lando (Intro, n 6) 587.

main performance of the contract he is getting into, without having to pay the costs of an in-depth analysis of all the contractual conditions, which perhaps concern very rare and marginal situations. A re-balancing of the parties' forces by means of an authoritative intervention limiting abusive and unfair contract terms would lead to more efficient contractual relations, reducing the final costs to the advantage of the whole market system.[50]

Protection measures for the benefit of an entrepreneur that is structurally in a subservient position may also be important to ensure the stability of an economic sector where typically economic power is unevenly distributed, such as the distribution chain.[51] This is what happens, for example, in the case of *subfornitura* in Italian law[52] and *sous-traitance* under French law.[53] Here the rules aim at avoiding the possibility that the exploitation of the strong party in a contractual chain may lead to the insolvency of the subcontractors, who are generally small or medium enterprises, generating risks for the firms in the chain, possibly for the whole economic system. This happens also for standard contract terms. If, in a certain branch of the market, general conditions are unfavourable for weak entrepreneurs (for example by making it very difficult for them to bring actions through a choice of forum clause naming a forum abroad or an amendment of the applicable law), this could lead in periods of economic crisis to an insolvency that would have been avoidable with more balanced general contract conditions.

On the other hand, one must consider that excessively protectionist and unjustifiably invasive legislation could create entrance barriers to certain markets. The subsequent cost increase could reduce the profit margin, thereby discouraging those who would be strong parties from entering that market.

All these arguments lead us to recognise that there is a need for a sophisticated and differentiated approach in regulating boilerplate in business transactions. The standard paradigm of transactions

---

50 Akerlof (Ch 1, n 6) 488ff.
51 Mogendorf (Intro, n 2) 23ff. Similarly Agrifoglio (Intro, n 14) 1370; Guido Alpa and Mads Andenas, *Fondamenti del diritto privato europeo* (Giuffrè 2005) 612ff (discussing in general the position of the SMEs on the market).
52 *Legge* 18 June 1998 no 192 *sulla disciplina della subfornitura nelle attività produttive*.
53 *Loi* no 75-1334 of 31 December 1975, according to which a subcontracting agreement stipulates that 'un entrepreneur confie par un sous-traité, et sous sa responsabilité, à une autre personne appelée sous-traitant l'exécution de tout ou partie du contrat d'entreprise ou d'une partie du marché public conclu avec le maître de l'ouvrage' (art 1).

traditionally underlying general contract law rules in fact considers business parties as individuals negotiating with equal bargaining powers in perfect markets. Such a model, however, fits very poorly in a system where relations are asymmetrical. Therefore, it is necessary to build a new legal structure addressing the phenomena and to try finding a fair balance in the regulation between the different interests at stake. A certain limitation of possible contracting with regard to the imposition of general conditions of contract seems appropriate.

3   Regulating asymmetrical b2b relationships

Signs of a new trend

The starting point of a modern positivist approach is that freedom – therefore also freedom for drafting the parties' own solution – needs a 'stable, continuous legal framework' where 'legal innovation and change' can then flourish.[1] Once assessed that weak professionals should be protected from unfair contract terms imposed on them by their stronger contractual parties, this means that the regulatory framework should provide for a clear identification of the situations deemed worthy of protection and of the tools to carry out this objective.

This is the direction taken by many law systems. Provisions were introduced that, albeit confined to specific sectors and to certain contractual relations, express the same general concern to prohibit excessive contractual imbalances of rights and obligations originating from power asymmetries in the negotiation phase. Thus, they aim at bringing the real market closer to the ideal market and, at the same time, at guaranteeing the justice of the individual relationship.

Indeed, some legislators started already in the 1960s and in the 1970s to identify situations of structural weakness of entrepreneurs deemed deserving of protection, and to draft protective rules. This is the case, for example, for the *franchisee* in the United States of America,[2] the

---

1 Joseph Raz, *Between Authority and Interpretation: On the Theory of Law and Practical Reason* (Oxford University Press 2009) 48. On these topics, see Stefan Grundmann, 'Three Views on Negotiation – An Essay between Disciplines', in Kai Purnhagen and Peter Rott (eds), *Varieties of European Economic Law and Regulation* (Springer 2014) 8.
2 The Federal Trade Commission promulgated in 1978 the Trade Regulation Rule Disclosure Requirements and Prohibitions Concerning Franchising and Business Opportunities Ventures – 16 C.F.R. 436.

subcontractor in the French legislation,[3] the German law on standard business terms of 1976,[4] and the Spanish rules on insurance, transport, and distribution contracts.[5] Other examples such as the paragraphs regulating the sales representative (*Handelsvertreter*, § 84ff HGB) in Germany or the Italian rules on incorporation and transparency in the negotiation of standard contract terms (arts 1341, 1342 cc) were even older.

Also the European legislator introduced sector-specific regulations of b2b contracts in which weaker party protection is the primary and direct purpose of the legislative intervention,[6] such as the Directive (EEC) 86/653 on commercial agents[7] or the Directive (EC) 00/35 on late payments in commercial transactions.[8] Considering the subjection of one entrepreneur to another, the economic consequences of exploitation are comparable to situations such as those of consumers or workers: there are market asymmetries that create inequality of bargaining power between a weak and a strong party. This imbalance is considered a threat for correct market relationships, so that rules are introduced for the protection of the business acting as the weaker party of the contract.

A partially different approach was adopted in the Nordic countries, whose legislations on the topic, having been influenced by the Nordic Contracts Act, share similar traits.[9] A general provision identifies

---

3 *Loi* n 75-1334 of 31 December 1975.

4 *Gesetz zur Regelung des Rechts der Allgemeinen Geschäftsbedingungen (AGB-Gesetz)* of 9 December 1976, BGBl I, 3317. It is well known that, after the *Schuldrechtsmodernisierung* of 2002 reforming and modernising the German law of obligations, its content was transferred in the §§ 307ff BGB, that were already discussed above; see Ch 1.2. 'Fairness Control in All B2B Contracts: the German Case'.

5 See more in detail Mato Pacin (Intro, n 24) 106ff with further references.

6 For a deeper discussion of the European legislation focusing on asymmetric contracts between a dominant business and another market player with inequality of bargaining power see Vincenzo Roppo, 'From Consumer Contracts to Asymmetric Contracts: A Trend in European Contract Law' (2009) European Review of Contract Law 304ff, who identifies a certain change in the European legislator's perspective in domains where he identifies the need to protect the weaker party and notices an increasingly noticeable shift towards a regulation of asymmetric contracts. See also Twigg-Flesner (Intro, n 14) 65ff.

7 Council Directive (EEC) 86/653 on the coordination of the laws of the Member States relating to self-employed commercial agents [1986] OJ L382/17 (Commercial Agents Directive).

8 European Parliament and Council Directive (EC) 2000/35 on combating late payment in commercial transactions [2000] OJ L200/35 (Late Payments Directive).

9 On this topic see Mads Bryde Andersen and Eric Runesson, 'An Overview of Nordic Contract Law', in Torgny Håstad (ed), *The Nordic Contracts Act* (DJØF Publishing 2015) 15ff.

unfair contract terms in consumer as well business contracts. As for the latter, relevant for the protection of one of the parties is the identification of her weak position in the relation with the counterparty, and it is left to the courts to ascertain on a case-by-case basis if the relation between the parties is asymmetrical.

Section 36 of the Danish Act on Contracts (LBK n 781 af 16/8/1996) provides a general clause allowing to amend or disregard terms that are unreasonable or contrary to honest conduct, taking into account the circumstances of the conclusion of the agreement, the content of the agreement, and other circumstances.[10] This provision is mainly applied as a protection for the weak party in a contract: when applied to contracts between professionals,[11] consideration has to be taken of the resources each party has in terms of preparing, negotiating, and foreseeing the consequences of the contract she is about to stipulate. Accordingly, whether a standard term is to be considered unreasonable in a business contract varies and is not a fixed standard. What should be held unreasonable for a weak party such as a consumer or a small business may not be considered as such when it is offered to a strong party such as a big corporation. Between two powerful professional parties even highly unreasonable consequences of a contract are unlikely to be disregarded by a judge pursuant to § 36. A party with strong resources and legal counsel is assumed to know the risk and foresee the consequences of the contracts she is negotiating.

Similarly, in Finland the Act on the regulation of contract terms between businesses (1062/1993) provides a protection from unfair contract terms only if the business parties' position is unequal and the weaker party is in need of special protection, recognising clearly that the concept of weaker party is relative.[12] The absolute size of the weaker parties is not relevant in itself, but only in comparison with that of the counterparty (see also Finnish Government Bill 93/1993).

---

10 'An agreement may be amended or set aside wholly or in part if it will be unfair or inconsistent with honest conduct to claim the agreement. The same applies to other legal transactions. 2. Decisions made under subsection 1 must take into account the circumstances at the conclusion of the agreement, the substance of the agreement and subsequent circumstances'. A translated version of the provision is available in Frants Dalgaard-Knudsen, *Danelaws on Contracts. Principles, Practices and Law Today* (Danelaws 2015) 128.
11 For unfair consumer agreements see Section 38 c.
12 As reported by Johan Bärlund, 'Protection of the Weaker Party in B2B Relations in Nordic Contract Law', in Torgny Håstad (ed), *The Nordic Contracts Act* (DJØF Publishing 2015) 96.

An indication that the concept of weaker party is relative to specific contractual relations is also clear in Sec 36 of the Swedish Contracts Act 1915:218[13] as well as in Sec 2 of the Swedish Act on Contract Terms between Businesses 1984:292.

Indeed, in more recent years, even in Member States where there is no general provision for substantive control over standard contract terms between professional parties certain partial regulations have been emerging dealing with situations in which both parties are entrepreneurs, and which are intimately associated with assumptions of structural inequality between contractors. With greater or lesser progress, in most European countries[14] as well as in the European legislation[15] reform trends are underway, all having in common the understanding that consumers are not the only parties worthy of protection when discussing general contract terms. Even professionals are seen as the weak party in a standard negotiation.[16]

Nonetheless, nowadays it is not possible to recognise in the various legal systems common general figures or categories that would make a legal assessment possible, for example a recognised notion of the typical cases of subordination of one entrepreneur to another. Different regulatory techniques are used to protect a weak business party depending on the specific domain, so that it seems impossible to recognise general principles on this topic.

The issue of possible inconsistencies is particularly evident if one considers the Italian system and its different provisions protecting entrepreneurs and other professional parties from unfair contract terms. This gives rise to the doubt that the certainty of law and the predictability of the solutions which a judge could provide for other similar cases are undermined.

13 Expressly on this see the judgement of the Swedish Supreme Court NJA 1979, 483, as cited by Bärlund ibid 98f.
14 See for example in France the recent art 1171 *Code civil* as well as the newly revised L 442 of the commercial code. On this see above Intro, nn 22 and 23. Another (not so successful) example of this tendency is the Spanish legal system, where different reform projects were drafted to introduce in the general law of obligations and contracts forms of substantive control protecting weak parties; for specific references see Mato Pacin (Intro, n 24) 90ff.
15 Reference goes to the already-mentioned Dir 2019/633 on unfair trading practices in business-to-business relationships in the agricultural and food supply chain (Intro, n 30) and to the Reg 2019/1150 promoting fairness and transparency for business users of online intermediation services (Intro, n 31).
16 Along the same lines Roppo (Ch 3, n 6) 339ff.

Incorporation and transparency in the rules of the Italian *Codice Civile*

An analysis of the protection of business parties against unfair contract terms in Italy has to start from the rules of the *codice civile* of 1942, still significant in this context. From a regulatory perspective the first norms to consider are indeed arts 1341 and 1342 cc on unilaterally predisposed standard contract terms.[17]

These provisions on procedural fairness apply to uniform and pre-formulated terms that are meant to be used for an indefinite set of contracts, regardless if they are offered to consumers or to business parties,[18] as long as they have not been individually negotiated. As already discussed,[19] they set rules on transparency and incorporation in the adoption of standard contract terms. Moreover, they identify certain clauses that are considered unreasonably one-sided (commonly called '*clausole vessatorie*', literally meaning vexatious clauses) and need to be specifically agreed to in writing in order to be adopted as part of the contract. According to the established case law, the rules do not apply to contracts concluded by parties having the same bargaining power[20] that freely negotiated the terms of the contract,[21] nor to cases in which both parties spontaneously agreed to use a specific contractual scheme, considering it appropriate to define their interests in the contract.[22]

The rules provided in arts 1341 and 1342 cc represented an important innovation when they entered into force in 1942, because they recognised that very often the freedom of contract and the equality between contract parties – which represented the unexpressed assumption of all nineteenth-century codifications,[23] going back to the Kantian

---

17 On these provisions see page 27f.

18 See recently It Cass civ no 7605/2015; It Cass civ no 12153/2006; It Cass civ no 11757/2006; It Cass civ no 15385/2000. Moreover, Franco Carresi, 'Il contratto', in Piero Schlesinger (ed), *Trattato di diritto civile e commerciale Cicu-Messineo*, (Giuffré 1987) 219; Cesare Massimo Bianca, *Diritto civile*, (vol III, 'Il contratto', Giuffré 2000) 342ff; Rodolfo Sacco and Giorgio De Nova, 'Obbligazioni e contratti', in Pietro Rescigno (ed), *Trattato di diritto privato* (Utet 1999) 104.

19 See page 27.

20 It Cass civ no 6886/1987.

21 It Cass civ no 11757/2006; It Cass civ no 15385/2000; It Cass civ no 4847/1986.

22 It Cass civ no 136/1987.

23 It is well known that these codifications were imbued in a more or less conscious way of economic and political liberalism; see for all Franz Wieacker, *Das Sozialmodell der klassischen Privatrechtsgesetzbücher und die Entwicklung der modernen Gesellschaft* (Müller 1953) 9ff; Franz Wieacker, *Privatrechtsgeschichte*

conception of private law as the law of free determination between equals[24] – existed only formally and that in real transactions parties often fail to be on the same level and to have the same strength.[25] However, these provisions only stop at the level of advance disclosure rules. With time it became evident that they created a presumption of meaningful assent that in fact was not guaranteed. Italian courts were inflexible in their interpretation of the provisions: a double signature was considered enough and no form of *Inhaltskontrolle* following the German rules was ever allowed.[26] This way, it did not guarantee that the party assenting to the terms actually took notice and reviewed them, nor did it affect the length of standard forms. In practice, it was quite the opposite. Imposing no assessment on the content of the terms and setting no limits to permissible contracting, this provision soon showed that, though increasing transaction costs, it did not produce substantial benefits, so that the Directive (EC) 93/13 on unfair terms

---

der Neuzeit unter besonderer Berücksichtigung der deutschen Entwicklung (Vandenhoeck und Ruprecht 1967) 468ff. On the Italian *codice civile* see Luigi Mengoni, 'Forma giuridica e materia economica', in Domenico Pettiti (ed), *Studi in onore di Alberto Asquini* (vol III, Cedam 1963) 1075ff. On the German BGB see Ludwig Raiser, 'Vertragsfunktion und Vertragsfreiheit' in Ernst von Caemmerer et al. (eds), *100 Jahre Deutsches Rechtsleben – Festschrift zum hundertjährigen Bestehen des Deutschen Juristentags 1960–1960* (Müller 1960) 101ff, who already started questioning the exclusiveness of the *Willensdogma* in consideration of the social function of contractual freedom. These assumptions were also common in the area of common law – for an ample discussion see Kessler (Intro, n 11) 630:

> 'Since a contract is the result of the free bargaining of parties who are brought together by the play of the market and who meet each other on a footing of social and approximate economic equality, there is no danger that freedom of contract will be a threat to the social order as a whole.'

24 On liberty of contract as the guiding principle of private law see Immanuel Kant, *Metaphysik der Sitten* (vol I, Nicolovius 1797) 55ff.

25 'Libertà di contratto ed eguaglianza formale dei contraenti apparivano (allorché prevalevano le teorie economiche del laisser faire, laissez-passer) i presupposti non solo del conseguimento degli interessi particolari (dei contraenti), ma anche dell'interesse generale della società' Vincenzo Roppo, Il contratto (Il Mulino 1977) 34. On this topic see also Emanuela Navarretta, 'Principio di uguaglianza, principio di non discriminazione e contratto' (2013) Rivista di diritto civile 547ff.

26 Literature on this topic is very broad. See for all Bianca (Ch 3, n 18) 368ff; Mario Nuzzo, 'Condizioni generali di contratto', in Natalino Irti (ed), *Dizionario del diritto privato*, I, *Diritto Civile* (Giuffré 1980) 157ff; Giovanni Capo, 'La normativa sull'affiliazione commerciale e la tutela contrattuale dell'imprenditore "debole". Appunti per uno studio sulla disciplina della contrattazione "asimmetrica" tra imprese', in *Scritti in onore di Vincenzo Buonocore* (vol IV, Giuffré 2005) 4344f.

in consumer contracts was greeted with enthusiasm by courts as well as by scholars.[27]

These rules were transposed in 1996 and are currently set in arts 33ff of the so-called 'consumer code' (decreto legislativo 6 September 2005, no 206), which reorganised and collected in a comprehensive regulatory framework all the rules concerning consumer contracts that were otherwise scattered in different contexts. Accordingly, unfair terms that cause a significant imbalance of the rights and obligations arising from contracts are void in consumer contracts.[28]

However, no general application of the rules protecting consumers from unfair contract terms is allowed. As the position of the provisions in the Italian law system makes clear, the 'substantive' control on contract terms with an unfairness test is restricted to b2c relations. Although many scholars consider it irrational to distinguish cases with identical information asymmetries and interests at stake and therefore advocate for a wider application of the rules on unfair contract terms,[29] the case law[30] – following the lead of the ECJ that always advocated for an interpretation of the consumer concept in its strict sense[31] – has always been adamant when applying these rules. They

---

27 See Azzaro and Sirena (Intro, n 15) 43ff; Alpa and Patti (Intro, n 15) with further references.
28 For an analysis of these provisions see among others Salvatore Patti, 'Le condizioni generali di contratto e i contratti del consumatore', in Pietro Rescigno and Enrico Gabrielli, *Trattato dei contratti, I contratti in generale* (vol I, UTET 2006) 345ff with further references.
29 So Giuseppe Amadio, 'Il terzo contratto. Il problema', in Gregorio Gitti and Gianroberto Villa (eds), *Il terzo contratto* (Il Mulino 2008) 23f with further references.
30 It Cass civ no 15531/2011; It Cass civ no 21763/2013; It Cass civ no 5705/2014; It Cass civ no 17848/2017:
   'La qualifica di consumatore spetta solo alle persone fisiche, quindi non alle società, e la stessa persona fisica che svolga attività imprenditoriale e professionale potrà essere considerata alla stregua del semplice consumatore soltanto allorché concluda un contratto per la soddisfazione di esigenze della vita quotidiana estranee all'esercizio di dette attività.'
31 See among others ECJ 3 July 1997, Case C-269/95 *Benincasa* [1997] ECR I-3788, 3800, where the ECJ had to decide if a prospective franchisee should be qualified as professional or consumer in the moment she enters into the contract; it stated that a contract has a commercial nature if it concerns a prospective enterprise of a trade by one of the parties. For further rulings of the ECJ on the topic compare ECJ 14 March 1991, Case C-361/89 *Di Pinto* [1991] ECR I-1189; ECJ 19 January 1993, Case C-89-91 *Shearson Hutton* [1993] ECR I-139; ECJ 7 March 1998, Case C-45/96 *Dietzinger* [1996] ECR I-1199; ECJ 22 November 2001, Case C-541 and C-542/99 *Idealservice* [2001] ECR I-9049. Indeed, the European rules on unfair contract terms do not even apply – according to the ECJ – to a contract for the

can be used only to the protection of individuals, not companies, and to individuals who carry out entrepreneurial and professional activities only when they are entering into contracts for the satisfaction of needs of everyday life unrelated to the exercise of such activities. Even the Constitutional Court was called upon to rule on this topic and it did not consider it necessary to extend the scope of these rules in b2b relations, even when they are structurally or functionally asymmetrical.[32] Businesses are therefore excluded, even in those cases where there actually are imbalances in bargaining power.

The Italian legislator, however, has not been deaf to the needs of weak business parties, especially after the recent economic developments that, in the aftermath of the world financial crisis, have brought to light the importance of protecting small entrepreneurs and other business parties. Indeed, a recent interesting trend in the legislation goes in the direction of defending these professionals with the means of considerably influencing the freedom of contract of their strong counterparties.[33] In these provisions, that to some extent might be considered *avant-garde* when expressing a general direction in the legislation, the existence of an imbalance situation between powers is generally assessed on the basis of specific contract types, so that an evaluation of the actual exploitation of one party's weakness and the recognition of a real imbalance are not requested.

Enacting rules on substantive fairness

Mandatory rules for the protection of weaker professionals from unfair clauses can of course be found in the legislation combating late payments in commercial transactions (art 7 d lgs 9 October 2002 no 231, implementing Dir 2000/35, subsequently amended by d lgs 9 November 2012 no 192 implementing Dir 2011/7) that is common to all EU Member States. Small and medium-sized enterprises indeed have a high risk of bankruptcy because of delays in the payments for their

---

supply of goods that are meant to be used partly (60%) for the buyer's personal purposes and partly (40%) for business purposes, so ECJ 20 January 2005, Case C-464/01 *Gruber* [2005] ECR I-439.

32 Corte cost 22 November 2002, no 469, in Corriere giuridico (2003) 1005ff and It Cass civ ord 11 October 2002 no 14561.

33 On this topic see for all Vincenzo Roppo, 'Contratto di diritto comune, contratto del consumatore, contratto con asimmetria di potere contrattuale: genesi e sviluppi' (2001) Rivista di diritto privato 769ff; Giovanni Capo, *Attività di impresa e formazione del contratto* (Giuffré 2001) 188ff with further references.

invoices. The challenge posed by the payment practices of stronger operators became even more prominent as credit lines and bank loans became less available following the latest world financial crisis.[34] Such practices put them in a position subordinate to the debtor, since their existence depends on the regularity and timeliness of payments. As imposed by art 7 Dir 2011/7,[35] the Italian legislation prohibits the abuse of freedom of contract to the disadvantage of the creditor, who might not be in a position to negotiate fair agreements as regards payments.[36]

According to art 7 d lgs 9 October 2002 no 231 on late payments in commercial transactions, also applicable to self-employment,[37] a contract term relating to the payment deadline, the rate of interest for late payment or the compensation for recovery costs is unenforceable if it is grossly unfair to the creditor. Judges can *ex post* scrutinise the conditions the parties agreed to, taking into account any gross deviation from good commercial practices, contrary to good faith and fair dealing. Specific limitations are stated in *comma* 3 and 4: a term is always void if it excludes interest for late payment or compensation for recovery costs.

In these cases, it is noteworthy that the scrutiny of a judge may be followed by a replacement of the private ordering: if a court finds that an unfair term in a commercial transaction is void, it can directly modify the contract by revising the content of that term, replacing it with the terms (for example regarding the payment period) provided by the law.[38]

---

34 This was specifically stated by the European Commission https://ec.europa.eu/growth/smes/support/late-payment accessed 28 April 2019.

35 See also the Recital 28, Dir 2011/7.

36 For an analysis of this provision see among others Alberto Maria Benedetti, 'La nullità delle clausole derogatorie', in Alberto Maria Benedetti and Stefano Pagliantini (eds), *La nuova disciplina dei ritardi di pagamento nelle transazioni commerciali* (Giappichelli 2013) 89; Teresa Pasquino, 'D lgs 9 ottobre 2002, n. 231 (come modificato dal d lgs 9 novembre 2012 no 192)', in Enrico Gabrielli (ed), *Commentario del codice civile, Delle obbligazioni* (UTET 2013) 688ff.

37 This is provided by art 2 *legge* 22 May 2017 no 81. On this topic see Matteo Mattioni, 'La tutela del lavoro autonomo nelle transazioni commerciali e le clausole e le condotte abusive', in Gaetano Zilio Grandi and Marco Biasi (eds), *Commentario breve allo statuto del lavoro autonomo e del lavoro agile* (Giuffré 2018) 265ff.

38 This provision has been very much discussed. On this topic see Benedetti (Ch 3, n 36) 101ff; Pasquino (Ch 3, n 36) 688ff; Stefano Pagliantini, 'Profili sull'integrazione del contratto abusivo parzialmente nullo', in Giovanni D'Amico and Stefano Pagliantini (eds), *Nullità per abuso ed integrazione del contratto* (Giappichelli 2013) 67ff; Valentina Cuocci, 'Brevi note sulla direttiva comunitaria relativa ai ritardi di pagamento nelle transazioni commerciali e sulla sua attuazione in Germania' (2006) Contratto e impresa/Europa 349ff with further references.

Apart from these provisions deriving from European secondary law, a first set of mandatory rules restricting permissible contracting in b2b situations and striking down unconscionable terms and provisions can be found in the law of 1998 regulating subcontracting agreements (*subfornitura*), a contractual model often used for outsourcing or in vertically integrated production chains.[39] This contractual scheme is generally used by a big company in order to entrust the execution of a productive phase to an independent contractor, so that they are characterised by a manifest economic advantage of one party over the other and by strong information asymmetries. Such a configuration typically brings about the superiority of one party over the other as regards their relative bargaining power.[40]

This set of rules includes a provision prohibiting the abuse of economic dependence (art 9) which in its *comma* 3 states that the agreement achieving an abuse of the economic dependence of one firm is void.[41] Economic dependence is defined here as a situation in which a firm can determine, in its contractual relations with another firm, a disproportionate inequality of rights and obligations, also considering the actual possibilities for the weaker firm to find satisfactory alternatives on the market.[42]

---

39 *Legge* 18 June 1998 no 192 *sulla disciplina della subfornitura nelle attività produttive*. For a discussion of this regulatory framework and of subcontracting in general see Angelo Bertolotti, *Il contratto di subfornitura* (UTET 2000) 178ff; Francesco Prosperi, *Il contratto di subfornitura e l'abuso di dipendenza economica* (ESI 2002) with further references. It is well known that these rules rely heavily on the already-mentioned French legislation on the *sous-traitance* (*Loi* no 75-1334 of 31 December 1975, see n 149).

40 On this topic see among others Luca Renna, 'L'abuso di dipendenza economica come fattispecie transtipica' (2013) Contratto e impresa 375ff.

41 On the complex drafting process of this provision see Maria Rosaria Maugeri, *Abuso di dipendenza economica e autonomia privata* (Giuffrè 2003) 1ff; Colangelo (Ch 2, n 23) 63ff with further references. For a specific application of this provision in the case law see Trib Massa ord 26 February 2014 and ord 15 May 2014 in (2015) La Nuova Giurisprudenza Civile Commentata 218ff.

42 Literature on the topic is very broad; see lately Angelo Barba, *Studi sull'abuso di dipendenza economica* (Wolters Kluwer-Cedam 2018); Francesco Macario, 'Genesi, evoluzione e consolidamento di una nuova clausola generale: il divieto di abuso di dipendenza economica' (2016) Giustizia civile 506ff; Vittorio Bachelet, 'La clausola squilibrata è nulla per dipendenza economica e il prezzo lo fa il giudice' (2015) La Nuova Giurisprudenza Civile Commentata 225ff; Mario Libertini, 'La responsabilità per abuso di dipendenza economica: la fattispecie' (2013) Contratto e impresa 1ff; Renna (Ch 3, n 40) 370ff; Philipp Fabbio, *L'abuso di dipendenza economica* (Giuffré 2006) 35ff; Cristoforo Osti, *Nuovi obblighi a contrarre* (Giappichelli 2004) 243ff.

The provision applies to all other asymmetrical contractual relations such as franchising, leasing, supply contracts, etc.,[43] so that it is generally agreed upon that – also in consideration of the fact that Italian competition law in its strict sense[44] has no corresponding general prohibition of abuse of dominant position[45] – this rule sets a cross-sector principle ('a general clause') for any asymmetrical b2b relation characterised by the superior bargaining power of one party.[46]

43 See among others Macario (Ch 3, n 42) 509ff; Ernesto Capobianco, 'L'abuso di dipendenza economica. Oltre la subfornitura' (2012) Concorrenza e mercato 619ff; Elena La Rosa, *Tecniche di regolazione del contratto e strumenti rimediali* (Giuffrè 2012) 114; Vincenzo Pinto, 'L'abuso di dipendenza economica "fuori dal contratto" tra diritto civile e diritto antitrust' (2000) Rivista di diritto civile 400; Maugeri (Ch 3, n 41) 131ff; Capo (Ch 3, n 26) 4299ff and 4345ff; Lorenzo Delli Priscoli, 'Il divieto di abuso di dipendenza economica nel franchising, fra principio di buona fede e tutela del mercato' (2006) Giurisprudenza di merito 2153ff; Fabbio (Ch 3, n 42) 102ff; Marco Saverio Spolidoro, 'Riflessioni critiche sul rapporto tra abuso di posizione dominante e abuso dell'altrui dipendenza economica' (1999) Rivista di diritto industriale I 195ff. In the recent case law see It Cass civ no 25606/2018; It Cass civ no 16787/2014; It Cass civ, *sezioni unite*, no 24906/2011; Trib Roma 24 January 2017, no 1239 *DeJure*; Trib Milano 6 December 2017 *Contratti* 2018, 424; Trib Milano 17 June 2016 *Foro italiano* (2016) I 3636. For the opposite view see however Alberto Musso, 'La subfornitura', in Antonio Scialoja and Giuseppe Branca (eds), *Commentario del codice civile* (Zanichelli 2003) 483ff and in the case law Trib Roma 17 March 2010, as well as 19 February 2010, 24 September 2009, and 5 May 2009, all in Foro italiano (2011) I 255ff; Trib Bari ord 2 July 2002 Foro italiano (2002) I 3208.

44 Another controversial issue is the complex nature (one might say 'double soul') of the provision prohibiting the abuse of economic dependence. Indeed, it is set at the crossroad between antitrust and contract law and it combines the aims of competition law with core principles of contract theory such as good faith and abuse of rights. On this topic see especially Fabbio (Ch 3, n 42) 23ff and especially 35ff; Colangelo (Ch 2, n 23) 13f; Francesco Macario, 'Equilibrio delle posizioni contrattuali ed autonomia privata nella subfornitura', in Lanfranco Ferroni (ed), *Equilibrio delle posizioni contrattuali ed autonomia privata* (ESI 2002) 156ff; Angelo Barba, 'L'abuso di posizione dominante: profili generali', in Vincenzo Cuffaro (ed), *La subfornitura nelle attività produttive* (ESI 1998) 300ff with further references. For an analysis on a case-by-case basis see Libertini (Ch 2, n 21) 557ff.

45 Differing in this respect from the German and the French legislation (respectively, § 20 GWB and art L 420-2 *code de commerce*), even though these rules were important references in the drafting of the Italian provision on the abuse of economic dependence. On this see Maugeri (Ch 3, n 41) 3, 23ff; Osti (Ch 3, n 42) 249ff.

46 Renna (Ch 3, n 40) 390ff with further references also in case law; Macario (Ch 2, n 19) 313f; Macario (Ch 3, n 42) 509ff; Colangelo (Ch 2, n 23); Silvia Benucci 'La dipendenza economica nei contratti tra imprese', in Giuseppe Vettori (ed), *Equilibrio e usura nei contratti* (Cedam 2002) 218; Roberto Caso and Roberto Pardolesi, 'La nuova disciplina del contratto di subfornitura (industriale): scampolo di fine millennio o prodromo di tempi migliori?' (1998) Rivista di diritto privato 733ff. From a comparative perspective, this is also the case in other legal systems, such as

It even applies to professionals who depend economically on single clients.[47] One can therefore consider it a general clause in the Italian law system which prohibits the imposition of unjustifiably vexatious contractual conditions, thus setting mandatory restrictions on contracting.[48] Accordingly, any term making it possible for one party to unjustly exploit a hold-up situation where the counterparty made relationship-specific investments is void.

Such a rule allows the courts to control pervasively the content of the agreements between firms in order to protect the weaker party. They can judge the core of the contractual agreement, going much beyond its surface: in their evaluation they are free to consider both the economic aspects and the normative contents of the contract. They can declare void any unfair term that forces on the weaker party obligations, constraints, or costs that are unfair compared to the advantages attributed to the stronger party and of course they can award compensation for damages.[49]

It is generally in the interest of the business parties, especially of the weak one, to preserve the contract even if it is partially void. The threat of the termination of the business relation with the stronger party might indeed restrain the weaker party from challenging an unfair term. Accordingly, one might consider if the judge should be allowed to intervene on the contract by replacing the terms declared void according to art 9 *comma* 3, as is provided for terms on the payment deadline that are ineffective according to art 7 d lgs 231/2002. However, there might not be default provisions outlining how to

---

Germany or France, that served as models for the Italian legislator; see § 20 (2) 1 GWB; art 8 no 2, *Ordonnance no* 86–1243.

47 See, explicitly, art 3 *comma* 4 of *legge* 22 May 2017 no 81. On this topic see especially Barba (Ch 3, n 42) 149ff; Pietro Paolo Ferraro, 'Le professioni intellettuali e abuso di dipendenza economica' (2018) Corriere giuridico 217ff; Gionata Cavallini, 'Il divieto di abuso di dipendenza economica e gli strumenti del 'nuovo' diritto civile a servizio del lavoro autonomo', in Gaetano Zilio Grandi and Marco Biasi (eds), *Commentario breve allo statuto del lavoro autonomo e del lavoro agile* (Giuffré 2018) 265ff. This was generally recognised by scholars even before this provision came into force, but the courts never had the chance to tackle the problem; see Enrico Minervini, *L'equo compenso degli avvocati e degli altri liberi professionisti* (Giappichelli 2018) 11; Adalberto Perulli, 'Il jobs act degli autonomi: nuove (e vecchie) tutele per il lavoro autonomo non imprenditoriale' (2017) Rivista italiana di diritto del lavoro 185ff.

48 Among others see explicitly Macario (Ch 2, n 19) 313f; Macario (Ch 3, n 42) 509ff; Capobianco (Ch 3, n 43) 619ff.

49 For a deeper analysis of the remedies see for all Fabbio (Ch 3, n 42) 481ff; Musso (Ch 3, n 43) 529ff with further references.

replace the void term, as is the case for the rules on late payments, and the stronger party may easily argue that she would not have entered into the contract without the term declared void, and this might lead to the invalidity of the whole contract.[50] A judge's intervention might therefore inflict a deeper wound to the *synallagma* than the one he was trying to avoid by removing the unfair term.[51]

There are different proposals to solve this problem, such as resorting to the rules on consumer contracts (especially art 36 *codice del consumo* and, more in general, the rules on the so-called *nullità di protezione*) or arguing for the disapplication of the general rule in consideration of the *ratio* of the prohibition and the interests of the weaker party it is meant to protect.[52] The case law only occasionally addressed the problem and the judges, while intervening directly on the contractual clauses, argued taking into account the interest of the weaker party to continue the contractual relations with the strong party on fair and non-discriminatory terms.[53]

The form of private enforcement that was just discussed provided by comma 3 goes hand in hand with a form of public enforcement. Indeed, starting from 2001 the Italian Antitrust Authority (*Autorità garante per la concorrenza e il mercato*) can intervene sanctioning with warnings and fines parties abusing of another's economic dependence with agreements that may have an impact on fair competition and the markets. This is provided by art 9 *comma 3-bis*, also applying to the continued use of grossly unfair contractual terms that allow late payment in contravention of d lgs 231/2002.[54] These rules have

---

50 The relevant general provision, art 1419 cc, states indeed that the voidness of single terms, as long as they are not automatically replaced by legal provisions (*comma* 2), entails the voidness of the whole contract if one of the parties can prove that she would not have entered into that contract without the part which is affected (*comma* 1).

51 On this topic see specifically, among others, Bachelet (Ch 3, n 42) 222ff; Fabbio (Ch 3, n 42) 490ff; Fabbio, 'Abuso di dipendenza economica', in Antonio Catricalà and Enrico Gabrielli (eds), *I contratti della concorrenza*, *Trattato dei contratti* directed by Pietro Rescigno and Enrico Gabrielli (UTET 2011) 305f and 310f; Maugeri (Ch 3, n 41) 158ff; Musso (Ch 3, n 43) 537f.

52 Reference here goes to different possible arguments such as those retrieved from the German discussion on the *teleologische Reduktion* or on *quantitative Teilnichtigkeit*. On this problem see in detail Fabbio (Ch 3, n 42) 492ff; Maugeri (Ch 3, n 41) 158ff; Bachelet (Ch 3, n 42) 227ff with further references.

53 Trib Massa ord 26 February 2014 and ord 15 May 2014 both in (2015) La Nuova Giurisprudenza Civile Commentata 218ff.

54 See *Autorità Garante della Concorrenza e del Mercato*, *provv* 23 November 2016, no 26251, with comments by Valerio Cosimo Romano, 'Problemi scelti in tema

been very efficient and useful in order to guarantee a proper functioning of the markets, while at the same time protecting structurally
dependent firms.[55]

Recent developments in the Italian legislation

Only in more recent years, however, one may truly identify a legislative
tendency that seems to recognise in the consumer protection the model
for a sort of 'statute for the weaker party', that is then distinguished in
consideration of the peculiar aspects of weakness characterising the
single cases.[56]

Firstly, as provided by art 8 *legge* 24 March 2012 no 27, the scope
of the rules on unfair trading practices in arts 18ff *codice del consumo*
was expanded in order to include micro enterprises. It was considered
that although they carry out entrepreneurial and professional activities, these particularly small firms[57] need to be protected from more
sophisticated counterparties. Following indications coming from the
European institutions, this category of enterprises, considered 'particularly important for the development of entrepreneurship and job
creation',[58] was given the same protection as consumers.[59]

Such an alignment of b2c and b2b rules, however, is only excep-
tional.[60] It does not include small or medium-sized enterprises, even
though they are all equally considered in the Commission recommendation of 6 May 2003 defining these concepts and even though, as

---

di abuso di dipendenza economica da ritardo nei pagamenti commerciali' (2017)
Danno e responsabilità 380ff.

55 Renna (Ch 3, n 40) 374ff.
56 Minervini (Ch 3, n 47) 12ff.
57 According to art 18 *comma* 1 lett *d-bis* a micro enterprise is an entity, a company,
or an organisation, irrespective of its legal form, engaged in an economic activity, including self-employment and family businesses, that employs fewer than ten
persons and has an annual turnover and/or annual balance sheet total that does
not exceed two million euro (see also art 2 *comma* 3 Annex to the Commission
recommendation of 6.5.2003, concerning the definition of micro, small, and medium-
sized enterprises).
58 See Recital 8 Commission recommendation of 6.5.2003 concerning the definition
of micro, small, and medium-sized enterprises.
59 Daniela Valentino, 'Timeo Danaos et dona ferentes. La tutela del consumatore e
delle microimprese nelle pratiche commerciali scorrette' (2013) Rivista di diritto
civile 1157ff and 1168ff with further references.
60 Stefano Pagliantini, 'Il nuovo regime della trasparenza nella direttiva sui servizi
di pagamento' (2009) I Contratti 1165ff; Stefano Pagliantini, 'Per una lettura
dell'abuso contrattuale: contratti del consumatore, dell'imprenditore debole e della
microimpresa' (2010) Rivista di diritto commerciale I 409ff.

argued above, the relativity of the concept of weakness entails that small and medium-sized businesses may need the same protection as micro enterprises The concept of 'weak entrepreneur' according to Italian law has therefore to undergo a process of stratification into different sub-categories, each one characterised by its own protection regime, so that one has to carefully determine the status of the parties to asymmetric negotiations.

This emerges again when considering the recent rules on self-employment in *legge* 22 May 2017 no 81. This text introduces new measures aiming at the protection of independent contractors and other professionals as well as at encouraging flexible work environments. It contains, among others, specific provisions dealing with the substantive fairness of the contracts that are stipulated by such business parties: art 3 *comma* 1 and 2 states that certain terms cause a substantial imbalance in the contractual relations, so that they are to be considered unfair. They are not binding, and they give rise to liability. The rules, indeed, introduce an *ex post* scrutiny as well as a claim for damages.[61] This list includes clauses that enable the customer to alter unilaterally the contract terms or to terminate a long-term contract without reasonable notice, as well as clauses that fix a payment period longer than 60 calendar days.

Apart from the inconsistencies with other provisions (such as the legislation opposing late payments in commercial transactions as regards the payment period), these rules, which clearly recall the provisions on unfair terms in consumer contracts, introduce limits to permissible contracting only in those cases where the weak party is a self-employed professional. Entrepreneurs are explicitly excluded from the scope of the legislation according to art 1 *legge* 22 May 2017, no 81, bringing us to wonder if this may not breach the constitutional principle of equal treatment (art 3 Cost it).

The newly inserted art 13-*bis legge* 31 December 2012, no 247[62] on fair remuneration and unfair contract terms for lawyers (the so-called

---

61 See Perulli (Ch 3, n 47) 173ff; Perulli, 'Le tutele civilistiche: il ritardo nei pagamenti; le clausole e condotte abusive', in Luigi Fiorillo and Adalberto Perulli (eds), *Il jobs act del lavoro autonomo e del lavoro agile* (Giappichelli 2018) 27ff; Mattioni (Ch 3, n 37) 275ff; Ferraro (Ch 3, n 47) 217ff.

62 This provision was inserted in the law regulating the lawyers' profession by art 19-*quaterdecies decreto legge* 16 October 2017 no 148 that was converted into *legge* 4 December 2017 no 172 e subsequently modified by art 1 *comma* 487 *legge* 27 December 2017 no 205. On the very tormented legislative process that led to these provisions see Remo Danovi, 'L'onorario dell'avvocato tra parametri ed equo compenso' (2018) Corriere giuridico 589ff.

equo compenso avvocati) is even more insightful. Despite its very specific heading, this provision does not apply only to contracts stipulated by lawyers (also those working in partnerships or professional organisations) but also to all other self-employed professionals, when their contractual parties are strong clients such as banks, insurances, or big enterprises.[63] Art 13-*bis* presumes that in such relations clients overreach and take advantage of their dominant position, unilaterally imposing contract terms (*comma* 3), so that it sets specific standards for the remuneration (*comma* 2) as well as for the content of contract terms (*comma* 4–8). Entrepreneurs, instead, are again explicitly excluded from the scope of the provisions, so art 1 *legge* no 81/2017, as referred to by these rules.[64]

The substantive boundaries to permissible contracting concern terms undermining the core bargain between the professional and its strong client that are considered unfair and therefore void if they make the contract unreasonably one-sided to the detriment of the weak professional. Especially nine are listed in *comma* 5, constituting a 'black list' of unfair terms without a possibility of evaluation (*comma* 6): these range from terms allowing the client to alter unilaterally the contract (*a*) or to claim additional services free of charge (*c*) to terms setting a payment period of 60 days (*f*) or imposing advance payment for administrative costs (*d*).

Moreover, and this is also a real novelty in the Italian regulatory framework, the boundaries to private contracting concern also the remuneration itself. *Comma* 2 considers the remuneration fair if it is proportionate taking into account 'the amount and the quality of the contracted work as well as the content and characteristics of the professional services, complying with the parameters set by the Ministry of Justice'. Judges are called upon to consider the bargain and to step in directly on it between the stronger and the weaker part, because the unfairness – and thus the iniquity of the contract – is also (but not only) assessed in consideration of a fair compensation, determined *ex ante* and on the basis of abstract considerations and parameters set authoritatively (such as the value of the claim).[65]

---

63 These are defined *a contrario* by the EC recommendation 2003/361.

64 Art 19-*quaterdecies comma* 2 *decreto legge* 16 October 2017 no 148 as subsequently modified by art 1 *comma* 487 *legge* 27 December 2017 no 205 extending the scope of the rules.

65 For these parameters, see *decreti* no 140/2012 for accountants, no 46/2013 for labour consultants (*consulenti del lavoro*), and no 55/2014 for lawyers.

As already mentioned, such a provision causes significant disruption. Indeed, it is well known that European rules on unfair terms in consumer contracts specifically state that the assessment of the unfair nature of the terms shall not relate 'to the adequacy of the price and remuneration, on the one hand, as against the services or goods supplies in exchange, on the other, in so far as these terms are in plain intelligible language' (art 4 subs 2 Directive 93/13, implemented in Italy in art 34 *comma* 2 *codice del consumo*).[66] Despite the similarities in structure with the rules on consumer contracts and despite the identity of the terms and concepts used, these provisions are indeed quite unique in their normative content.

Some considerations on the Italian system

The image emerging from this brief and synthetical description is that of a very fragmented regulatory context with specific sectoral rules providing substantive boundaries over standard contracting and inconsistent lists of unfair terms that sometimes leave the possibility of evaluation, sometimes do not. In some of these provisions only professionals who prove to be in a weak and exploitable position are protected, in others the asymmetry is presumed *iuris et de iure* given a certain situation determined by the legislator.

Notwithstanding, some scholars are inclined to recognise significative systematic repercussions in these legislative processes. They identify in rules such as these a new contractual paradigm for asymmetrical b2b relations. The model they thus outline is conceived as significantly different from the one shaped by general contract law and traditionally provided in the *codice civile*. It would include the whole sphere of relations between professionals where unsophisticated parties are involved and where one party has very little or no bargaining power, recognising in these cases the consequences of physiological

---

66 On this topic see especially It Cass civ no 21600/2013; It Cass civ no 19559/2015; It Cass civ no 15408/2016:
   'il controllo giudiziale sul contenuto del contratto stipulato con il consumatore (...) è circoscritto alla componente normativa del contratto stesso, mentre è preclusa ogni valutazione afferente le caratteristiche tipologiche e qualitative del bene o del servizio fornito, o l'adeguatezza tra le reciproche prestazioni, richiedendosi soltanto che l'oggetto del contratto e il corrispettivo pattuito siano individuati in modo chiaro e comprensibile.'
   Cf Guido Alpa, 'L'equo compenso per le prestazioni professionali forensi' (2018) La Nuova Giurisprudenza Civile Commentata 716ff.

market situations, not of pathological elements depending on the subjective features of the real contractual relations.[67] The discussion on the so-called *terzo contratto* – 'third contract' for b2b transactions, as opposed to a 'first contract' that is individually negotiated by the parties on an equal basis, according to 'classic' contract law, and a 'second contract' for b2c transactions – is by now quite broad.[68]

These authors identify a common thread governing the area of business contracting in asymmetric situations especially in the following normative texts: the legislation on subcontracting and on the abuse of economic dependence, the regulation on late payments, and the rules on franchising.[69] They then extend these principles to all other cases, even if they are not directly considered in the specific scope of the regulations.

If one considers in detail the area at stake, this solution seems highly hypothetical and unrealistic. The different legal rules in question can be considered as traces of legislation prohibiting the abuse of one party over the other in asymmetrical situations, but they do not share the same rationale. Sometimes the protection is granted in consideration of the subjective status of the parties involved on the basis of their size alone (this is the case for example when one considers the rules protecting micro enterprises), sometimes in view of the particular content of the contractual agreement, regardless of the characteristics of

---

67 See especially Roppo (Ch 3, n 33) 786ff.

68 This phrase was proposed by Roberto Pardolesi, 'Prefazione', in Colangelo (Ch 2, n 23), XIII. For a critical discussion of the issues involved and further references, see Vincenzo Roppo, 'Parte generale del contratto, contratti del consumatore e contratti asimmetrici (con postilla sul "terzo contratto")' (2007) Rivista di diritto privato 679ff; Roppo 'Dal contratto del consumatore al contratto asimmetrico (schivando il 'terzo contratto')?', in Giuseppe Vettori (ed), *Remedies in Contract* (Cedam 2008) 221ff; Giuseppe Amadio, 'Nullità anomale e conformazione del contratto (note minime in tema di 'abuso dell'autonomia contrattuale')' (2005) Rivista di diritto privato 295ff; Amadio (n 178) 9ff; Amadio, 'Il contratto asimmetrico: l'ipotesi del terzo contratto', in *Lezioni di diritto civile* (Giappichelli 2018) 139ff; Giovanni D'Amico, 'La formazione del contratto', in Gitti and Villa (Ch 3, n 29) 37ff and especially 41ff; Andrea Zoppini, 'Il contratto asimmetrico tra parte generale, contratti di impresa e disciplina della concorrenza' (2008) Rivista di diritto civile I 536ff; Agrifoglio (Intro, n 14) 1374ff; Alberto Gianola, 'Terzo contratto' (2009) *Digesto delle discipline privatistiche, sezione civile*, agg IV, 571ff; Rosario Franco, *Il terzo contratto: da ipotesi di studio a formula problematica. Profili ermeneutici e prospettive assiologiche* (Wolters Kluver 2010) 35ff; Enrico Minervini, 'Il "terzo contratto"' (2009) I Contratti 493ff; Bianchini (Intro, n 17) 405ff.

69 *Legge* 6 May 2004, no 129. This regulation however does not include any provision on standard contract terms, so it was not relevant in this context. In franchising relationships, a protection is granted through art 9 *legge* no 192/1998 (see above).

the parties (eg in the regulations on late payments), sometimes considering both the contractual frame and the situation of the parties to it (so the prohibition of the abuse of economic dependence in the rules regulating subcontracting agreements).[70]

Even considering the rule on the abuse of economic dependence as the 'new emperor's clause',[71] it does not seem possible to recognise in the disjointed system of rules common legal categories such as, for example, a standard notion of subordination of one entrepreneur to another or a recognised notion of asymmetry in bargaining power.[72] Nor do the lists of unfair terms overlap. It is therefore impossible to reconstruct a general legal framework for the protection of weak business parties from unfair contract terms. There is indeed a resilient emergence of new and particular provisions regulating different areas in the economic life and one can actually identify several categories, all of which have a specific set of rules.[73]

However, this fragmentation does not exclude the application of common general rules. Even though the Italian legal system – like any other, especially as a consequence of the European sectoral interventions in the process of harmonising the Member States' national legal systems – shows tendencies that contradict to some extent its original aspiration to regulate contractual relations uniformly, the specific provisions do not cover all possible aspects and are therefore incomplete. This entails that each category should be considered separately when it comes to interpreting the respective rules and to filling their gaps. All the more reason for exercising caution when trying to excerpt from a special set of rules general principles considered applicable to other (maybe even all other) cases.[74]

De lege lata the protection of unsophisticated business parties needs significant improvement because it all depends on the

---

70 See also Macario (Ch 2, n 19) 288f and, more generally, Aurelio Gentili, 'I contratti di impresa e il diritto comune europeo' in Sirena (Ch 2, n 19) 108f.

71 So Pardolesi (Ch 3, n 68) XIV, who however acknowledges that it still does not have a clear imprinting but only a great unexplored potential.

72 For different definitions of asymmetrical contracts see, for example, Roppo, 'Dal contratto del consumatore al contratto asimmetrico' (Ch 3, n 68) 211, who puts an emphasis on the asymmetry of contractual power, and Amadio 'Il contratto asimmetrico' (Ch 3, n 68) 143ff who instead focuses on the aspect of economic dependence.

73 See especially Giorgio Cian, 'Dall'antica bipartizione "contratti civili-contratti commerciali" all'odierna pluripartizione dei rapporti obbligatori: valore sistematico ed ermeneutico di una classificazione per differenti discipline' in Sirena (Ch 2, n 19) 393ff.

74 Cian (Ch 3, n 73) 410.

specific scope of single isolated provisions, so that the certainty of law and the predictability of litigation's outcome are undermined. Nevertheless, the Italian example shows an interesting general tendency that matches a path trending also in the European legislation: here one can identify in recent legislative provisions the same intention of granting more protection to certain structurally weak positions in specific b2b situations such as the contractual relations in the food supply chain[75] and in the sale of online intermediation services.[76]

A central issue concerning the Italian rules, however, is related to the fragility of the Italian judicial system and the ineffectiveness of private enforcement. Small firms hardly assert their rights and claims, even when they are directly recognised by the law. Lawyers and other self-employed professionals tend as well to be reluctant to bringing an action before the courts, especially if this concerns their contractual relation with an important client because they fear they might lose that client. Provisions often turn out to be useless. Furthermore, it is not irrelevant that there is no clear and well-established case law in this matter that might render decisions more foreseeable. If we then take into account the well-known systemic slowness of the Italian Judiciary, it is unsurprising that these rules protecting small professionals have not had a significant impact in practice.

A perceptible change seems to have been brought about when a form of public enforcement through the Antitrust Agency was introduced for the abuse of economic dependence and for late payments (for both cases see art 9 *comma* 3-*bis legge* 18 June 1998, no 192).[77] When this public authority was granted a disciplinary power and sanctions for the infringement of the rules to the protection of the weak started to be enforced, these rules become effective.[78] Indeed, it should not be underestimated that the exacerbation of socio-economic differences and asymmetries on the market does not enhance competition. On the contrary, it only creates even stronger inequalities that force the weaker actors out of the market.

---

75 See the Directive (EU) 2019/633 (see above, Intro, n 30).

76 Regulation (EU) 2019/1150, see above, Intro, n 31.

77 This provision was added by art 11 *comma* 2 *legge* 5 May 2001 no 57 and later amended by art 10 *comma* 2 *legge* 11 November 2011 no 180.

78 See in particular *Autorità Garante della Concorrenza e del Mercato, provv* 23 November 2016, no 26251.

As far as the Italian system is concerned, the protection of weak business parties seems to have become more effective as a consequence of the enactment of a mixed system aiming at a good balance between public and private enforcement. It indeed tries to combine the protection of the damaged parties by means of private claims (aiming at declaring certain terms void and allowing a compensation for damages) with fines and other means in order to guarantee the compliance by the stronger parties.

Conclusions

The response to the challenges posed by unfair standard contract terms in business contracts must embed policy decisions fully aware of the legal and social contexts. Specifically, standard contract terms ought to be understood in the particular social context in which they operate, rather than in abstract terms.[1] Consumer and business contracts should not share the same regulation because the needs of protection are different. In particular, business contracts require differentiated solutions that should be adjusted to the individual circumstances of the case.[2] From a general point of view, however, some conclusions can be summed up.

Clarity and transparency of standard contract terms are paramount. This is a condition that has to be guaranteed for all business contracts, regardless of who is party to that contract. Terms should be formulated in a clear and comprehensible language and they should be easily available to the negotiating parties before they enter into a contract. Some parties, eg the more sophisticated ones and the repeat players, will be able to profit more than others from this requirement. Indeed, not all business parties, and especially not weak ones, may have the opportunity to negotiate the conditions that their stronger counterparties offer them, and to successfully change the boilerplate to their benefit. However, everyone should be put in a condition to read and understand the standard terms they are offered, so they can knowingly evaluate the possible benefits and disadvantages deriving from the contracts they are stipulating. Moreover, the transparency

---

1 'To understand boilerplate and to determine the law's proper response to it, one must approach it by building a structural model of how it is produced and used that goes beyond the model assumed in ordinary contract law', Rakoff (Ch 1, n 40) 200ff.
2 Similar conclusions but from a different perspective in Garvin (Ch 2, n 35) 385f, who argues in favour of developing different rules for small businesses in their contracts with consumers, with large firms, and with other small firms.

requirement is not invasive, as it does not entail unjustified transaction costs and it does not intervene on the substance of the contractual agreement. Therefore, freedom of enterprise remains untouched and, at the same time, freedom of contract can be exercised by both parties in effective and efficient ways.

Rules on substantive fairness for business contracts that establish limits to permissible contracting should be carefully weighted. A different regulation ought to be introduced bearing in mind the content of the terms in question as well as the parties to the respective contracts. It cannot be overlooked that the enactment of such rules inevitably involves a certain interference on the contents of the contracts, and therefore a constraint to the parties' freedom in shaping their contracts. Accordingly, it has to be taken with caution, in consideration of its objective content and of the subjective characteristics of persons involved. Indeed, the parties to business contracts are professionally involved so that none of them should be wholly exempt from the entrepreneurial risk that is naturally inherent in the activity they voluntarily and willingly decided to carry out. At the same time, their freedom in doing business should be restricted on a substantive level only when necessary and to the benefit of parties worthy of protection.

As far as the content of the terms in question is concerned, the Italian rules that limit the contractual autonomy of the parties in regard to the remuneration of self-employed professionals do not set a good example and should not be followed. In this regard, one ought to agree on the fact that conditions regarding the price and the main subject matter of the contract, as well as the adequacy of the remuneration agreed should not be subject to a fairness test, even if they are standardised, as long of course as they are stated in a clear and transparent way. All business parties are expected to be conscious of the main terms of the agreements they are entering into, and they are responsible for the choices they make when evaluating the core of the transaction. It is not disproportionate to ask of them to read the terms and fully understand their implications for the deal they are entering. They should be prepared to negotiate on the point.

More remains to be said about the remaining standard contents. Overall, a fairness test over boilerplate seems to be justified, at least when the bargaining parties do not work on an equal playing field. Restrictions and constraints to permissible contracting should not be set *a priori* for all business contracts, but only where the existence of an asymmetrical situation does not allow the parties to contract on an even footing. The relative concept of weak professional parties must also be taken into serious consideration.

Delimiting which business parties deserve to be protected from unfair standard terms is a demanding task and different elements should be evaluated and discussed to that end. A flexible approach seems certainly advisable, as there exists a great variety also among SMEs. Moreover, weakness in negotiations is a relative concept, to be assessed on a case-by-case basis in consideration of the relation between the parties to the contracts. One may agree on the fact that the position of the professionals in the market and their respective bargaining power have to be examined. The size of the contracting party is also relevant as an approximation of the weak position of one of the professionals in a negotiation. This is clearly evidenced by the current discussion in Germany, where the practice of introducing invasive forms of control over standard terms in b2b contracts is heavily criticised as it does not consider the relations existing between the parties. Moreover, the fact of a specific clause forming part of standard terms or being individually negotiated should definitely be central.

However, even though it is fundamental to give the appropriate weight to the need of protection of the weak business parties, this should not be the sole approach taken into view when assessing the right amount of judicial control for b2b contracts. Indeed, one ought to balance this perspective with a conflicting one, properly estimating the meaning of effective standardisation for the offering party in terms of enterprise organisation. To save transaction costs and due to the complex nature of their subject matter, a large share of business transactions depends heavily on preformulated contract terms offered by a party. The consideration of this 'enterprise perspective' entails a deeper understanding of the real meaning of standardisation in business transactions (and even of transactions in general) and it should not be left out of the picture.

Parties of equal strength are to be allowed to allocate the risks of their enterprise at their convenience, even if this distribution is unbalanced. If they have the choice to decide whether to make use of their contractual freedom, then they should bear the consequences stemming from it. This freedom should not be unlimited, but this is already recognised in every legal system that provides general rules that hold unenforceable grossly unjust terms that are against good faith and fair dealing.[3] It would be superfluous to provide with a formal enactment a specific discipline when this has already been encompassed in the general principles in force, which due to their width may be better tailored according to the specific case.

---

3 In Germany see §§ 138 and 242 BGB; in Italy see arts 1337 and 1375 cc.

Instead, when considering asymmetrical transactions where one party cannot recognise unfair contract terms or cannot protect himself against them through negotiations, a substantive control limiting permissible contracting is appropriate in order to avoid inefficiencies and unfairness. Size can be taken as a first approximation of asymmetry between the parties, but it should not be the only element taken into consideration for granting a substantive protection for one of the parties. Differences in bargaining power also depend on relative market power and sophistication. Weakness, moreover, should also be recognised when one of the parties to the contract, notwithstanding her size and position, is operating outside of her core business.

Abstract definitions of dependence based only on quantitative criteria and 'black' lists of unfair contract terms without a possibility of evaluation should be avoided. The rules should leave the judge with the possibility of considering the characteristics of the single case, evaluating the party's effective need for protection and the best solution for the case. Instead of black and grey lists, which bind an interpreter too strictly, a general clause seems to be preferable, and it should be one of fairness or reasonableness.

Otherwise, as the Italian example and the European legislation highlight, we go back to a regime based on the status of the parties, considering their professional role and their social and economic position, as well as their size, in order to identify the legal rules designed for their protection. Big, small, medium-sized, micro entrepreneurs, self-employed, consumers; all have their own legally relevant status, they are not a group but a class. Indeed, even though the codifications of the nineteenth-century Europe moved consciously away from a law based on status to a law based on contracts,[4] we can currently recognise a trend in the regulatory framework that enhances the notion of status with provisions that reflect the social and economic position of the contract's parties, so that contract law is deconstructed and then reshaped according to the different statutes with the scope of counterbalancing disparities and asymmetries.[5]

---

4 The codifications moved away from the 'stiffness of the status' to the 'mobility of the contract', so Pietro Rescigno, 'Premessa', in *Trattato di diritto dei contratti*, vol I, *I contratti in generale* (UTET 2006) XXXVIIff.

5 See also Renato Scognamiglio, 'Statuti dell'autonomia privata e regole ermeneutiche nella prospettiva storica e nella contrapposizione tra parte generale e disciplina di settore' (2005) Europa e diritto privato 1015ff. For a critical discussion on the current fragmentation of the law depending on the status of the parties and the deriving loss of coherence and unity of legal systems see Roppo (Ch 3, n 6) 344ff.

Literature

Agrifoglio, Giangabriele, 'Abuso di dipendenza economica e l'asimmetria nei contratti d'impresa (B2b)' (2008) Contratto e impresa 1356.

Akerlof, George A, 'The Market for "Lemons": Quality Uncertainty and the Market Mechanism' (1970) 84 QJ Economics 488.

Alpa, Guido, 'L'equo compenso per le prestazioni professionali forensi' (2018) La Nuova Giurisprudenza Civile Commentata 716.

Alpa, Guido and Andenas, Mads, *Fondamenti del diritto privato europeo* (Giuffrè 2005).

Alpa, Guido and Patti, Salvatore (eds), *Le clausole vessatorie nei contratti con i consumatori* (Giuffré 1997).

Amadio, Giuseppe, 'Il contratto asimmetrico: l'ipotesi del terzo contratto', in *Lezioni di diritto civile* (Giappichelli 2018).

Amadio, Giuseppe, 'Il terzo contratto. Il problema', in Gregorio Gitti and Gianroberto Villa (eds), *Il terzo contratto* (Il Mulino 2008).

Amadio, Giuseppe, 'Nullità anomale e conformazione del contratto (note minime in tema di 'abuso dell'autonomia contrattuale')' (2005) Rivista di diritto privato 295.

Azzaro, Andrea Mario and Sirena, Pietro, 'Il giudizio di vessatorietà delle clausole', in Enrico Gabrielli and Enrico Minervini (eds), *I contratti dei consumatori*, I (UTET 2005).

Bachelet, Vittorio, 'La clausola squilibrata è nulla per abuso di dipendenza economica e il prezzo lo fa il giudice: note a margine di un caso pilota' (2015) La Nuova Giurisprudenza Civile Commentata 222.

Barba, Angelo, 'L'abuso di posizione dominante: profili generali', in Vincenzo Cuffaro (ed), *La subfornitura nelle attività produttive* (ESI 1998).

Barba, Angelo, *Studi sull'abuso di dipendenza economica* (Wolters Kluver-Cedam 2018).

Bärlund, Johan, 'Protection of the Weaker Party in B2B Relations in Nordic Contract Law', in Torgny Håstad (ed), *The Nordic Contracts Act* (DJØF Publishing 2015).

Basedow, Jürgen, 'Vorbemerkung vor § 305', '§ 305', '§ 306', '§ 310', in Franz Jürgen Säcker, Roland Rixecker, Hartmut Oetker and Bettina Limperg (eds), *Münchener Kommentar zum BGB* (Beck 2019).

Beale, Hugh, 'The Role for European Contract Law: Uniformity or Diversity', in Francisco de Elizade (ed), *Uniform Rules for European Contract Law?* (Hart 2018).

Beale, Hugh, 'Unfair Terms in Contracts: Proposals for Reform in the UK' (2004) 27 Journal of Consumer Policy 289.

Beale, Hugh, Gullifer, Louise, and Paterson, Sarah, 'Ban on Assignment Clauses: Views from the Coalface' (2015) 3 JIBFL 463.

Beale, Hugh, Gullifer, Louise, and Paterson, Sarah, 'A Case for Interfering with Freedom of Contract? An Empirically-Informed Study of Bans on Assignment' (2015) Oxford Legal Studies Research Paper No 56/2015.

Bebchuk, Lucian A and Posner, Richard, 'One-Sided Contracts in Competitive Consumer Markets', in Omri Ben-Shahar (ed), *Boilerplate. The Foundation of Market Contracts* (Cambridge University Press 2007).

Becker, Felix, 'Die Reichweite der AGB-Inhaltskontrolle im unternehmerischen Geschäftsverkehr aus teleologischer Sicht' (2010) Juristenzeitung 1098.

Benedetti, Alberto Maria, 'La nullità delle clausole derogatorie', in Alberto Maria Benedetti and Stefano Pagliantini (eds), *La nuova disciplina dei ritardi di pagamento nelle transazioni commerciali* (Giappichelli 2013).

Ben-Shahar, Omri and White, James J, 'Boilerplate and Economic Power in Auto-Manufacturing Contracts', in Omri Ben-Shahar (ed), *Boilerplate. The Foundation of Market Contracts* (Cambridge University Press 2007).

Benucci, Silvia, 'La dipendenza economica nei contratti tra imprese', in Giuseppe Vettori (ed), *Equilibrio e usura nei contratti* (Cedam 2002).

Berger, Klaus P, 'Abschied von der Privatautonomie im unternehmerischen Geschäftsverkehr?' (2006) Zeitschrift für Wirtschaftsrecht 2149.

Berger, Klaus P, 'Für eine Reform des AGB-Rechts im Unternehmerverkehr' (2010) Neue Juristische Wochenschrift 467.

Berger, Klaus P, 'Schiedsgerichtsbarkeit und AGB-Recht', in Hans Schulte-Nölke, F Christian Genzow and Barbara Grunewald (eds), *Zwischen Vertragsfreiheit und Verbraucherschutz. Festschrift für Friedrich Graf von Westphalen* (Schmidt 2010).

Bertolotti, Angelo, *Il contratto di subfornitura* (UTET 2000).

Bianca, Cesare Massimo, *Diritto civile*, (vol III, 'Il contratto', Giuffré 2000).

Bianchini, Maurizio, La contrattazione d'impresa tra autonomia contrattuale e libertà di iniziativa economica (Part I, Giappichelli 2011).

Böhm, Franz, 'Das Problem der privaten Macht: ein Beitrag zur Monopolfrage' (1927/1928) Die Justiz 324, also in Ernst-Joachim Mestmäcker (ed), *Reden und Schriften über die Ordnung einer freien Gesellschaft, einer freien Wirtschaft und über die Wiedergutmachung* (Müller 1960) 25.

Böhm, Franz, 'Demokratie und ökonomische Macht', in Institut für Ausländisches und Internationales Wirtschaftsrecht (ed), *Kartelle und Monopole* (vol I, Müller 1961) 3.

Cafaggi, Fabrizio, 'Contractual Networks and the Small Business Act: Towards European Principles' (2008) European Review of Contract Law, 493.

Calnan, Richard, 'Ban the Ban: Prohibiting Restrictions on the Assignment of Receivables' (2018) 5 JIBFL 136.

Capo, Giovanni, *Attività di impresa e formazione del contratto* (Giuffré 2001).

Capo, Giovanni, 'La normativa sull'affiliazione commerciale e la tutela contrattuale dell'imprenditore "debole". Appunti per uno studio sulla disciplina della contrattazione 'asimmetrica' tra imprese', in *Scritti in onore di Vincenzo Buonocore* (vol IV, Giuffré 2005).

Capobianco, Ernesto, 'L'abuso di dipendenza economica. Oltre la subfornitura' (2012) Concorrenza e mercato 619.

Carresi, Franco, 'Il contratto', in Piero Schlesinger (ed), *Trattato di diritto civile e commerciale Cicu-Messineo* (Giuffré 1987).

Caso, Roberto and Pardolesi, Roberto, 'La nuova disciplina del contratto di subfornitura (industriale): scampolo di fine millennio o prodromo di tempi migliori?' (1998) Rivista di diritto privato 733.

Cavallini, Gionata, 'Il divieto di abuso di dipendenza economica e gli strumenti del 'nuovo' diritto civile a servizio del lavoro autonomo', in Gaetano Zilio Grandi and Marco Biasi (eds), *Commentario breve allo statuto del lavoro autonomo e del lavoro agile* (Giuffré 2018).

Cian, Giorgio, 'Dall'antica bipartizione "contratti civili-contratti commerciali" all'odierna pluripartizione dei rapporti obbligatori: valore sistematico ed ermeneutico di una classificazione per differenti discipline', in Pietro Sirena (ed), *Il Diritto Europeo dei contratti d'impresa* (Giuffrè 2006).

Coester, Michael, '§ 307', in Michael Martinek (ed), *J von Staudingers Kommentar zum BGB, Buch 2* (Sellier - de Gruyter 2013).

Coester-Waltjen, Dagmar, '§§ 308 and 309', in Michael Martinek (ed), *J von Staudingers Kommentar zum BGB, Buch 2* (Sellier - de Gruyter 2013).

Colangelo, Giuseppe, *L'abuso di dipendenza economica tra disciplina della concorrenza e diritto dei contratti. Un'analisi economica e comparata* (Giappichelli 2004).

Cuocci, Valentina, 'Brevi note sulla direttiva comunitaria relativa ai ritardi di pagamento nelle transazioni commerciali e sulla sua attuazione in Germania' (2006) Contratto e impresa/Europa 349.

D'Amico, Giovanni, 'La formazione del contratto', in Gregorio Gitti and Gianroberto Villa (eds), *Il terzo contratto* (Il Mulino 2008).

Dalgaard-Knudsen, Frants, *Danelaws on Contracts. Principles, Practices and Law Today* (Danelaws 2015).

Danovi, Remo, 'L'onorario dell'avvocato tra parametri ed equo compenso' (2018) Corriere giuridico 589.

Delli Priscoli, Lorenzo, 'Il divieto di abuso di dipendenza economica nel franchising, fra principio di buona fede e tutela del mercato' (2006) Giurisprudenza di merito 2153.

Drygala, Tim, 'Die Reformdebatte zum AGB-Recht im Lichte des Vorschlags für ein einheitliches europäisches Kaufrecht' (2012) Juristenzeitung 985.

Fabbio, Philipp, 'Abuso di dipendenza economica', in Antonio Catricalà and Enrico Gabrielli (eds), *I contratti della concorrenza, Trattato dei contratti* directed by Pietro Rescigno and Enrico Gabrielli (UTET 2011).

Fabbio, Philipp, *L'abuso di dipendenza economica* (Giuffré 2006).

Ferraro, Pietro Paolo, 'Le professioni intellettuali e abuso di dipendenza economica' (2018) Corriere giuridico 217.

Flume, Werner, *Allgemeiner Teil des Bürgerlichen Rechts*, 2, *Das Rechtsgeschäft* (4th ed, Springer 1992).

Franco, Rosario, *Il terzo contratto: da ipotesi di studio a formula problematica. Profili ermeneutici e prospettive assiologiche* (Wolters Kluver 2010).

Frenz, Walter, *Handbook of EU Competition Law* (Springer 2016).

Friedman, David D, 'Law as a Private Good' (1994) 10 Economics and Philosophy 319.

Galanter, Marc, 'Why the 'Haves' Come Out Ahead: Speculations on the Limits of Legal Change' (1974) 9 Law and Society Review 95.

Garvin, Larry T, 'Small Businesses and the False Dichotomies of Contract Law' (2005) 40 Wake Forest Law Review 29.

Genovese, Anteo, *Le condizioni generali di contratto* (Cedam 1954).

Gentili, Aurelio, 'I contratti di impresa e il diritto comune europeo', in Pietro Sirena (ed), *Il diritto Europeo dei contratti d'impresa* (Giuffrè 2006).

Gianola, Alberto, 'Terzo contratto' (2009) *Digesto delle discipline privatistiche*, *sezione civile*, agg IV, 571.

Gottschalk, Eckart, 'Das Trasparenzgebot und Allgemeine Geschäftsbedingungen' (2006) 206 Archiv für die civilistische Praxis 555.

Graf von Westphalen, Friedrich 'AGB-Kontrolle – Kein Standortnachteil' (2013) Betriebsberater 1357.

Graf von Westphalen, Friedrich, 'AGB-rechtliche Schutzschranken im unternehmerischen Verkehr: Rückblick und Ausblick' (2011) Betriebsberater 195.

Graf von Westphalen, Friedrich, '30 Jahre AGB-Recht – Eine Erfolgsbilanz' (2007) Zeitschrift für Wirtschaftsrecht 149.

Grundmann, Stefan, 'Three Views on Negotiation – An Essay Between Disciplines', in Kai Purnhagen and Peter Rott (eds), *Varieties of European Economic Law and Regulation* (Springer 2014).

Güners, Menderes and Ackermann, Tobias, 'Die Indizwirkung der §§ 308 und 309 BGB im unternehmerischen Geschäftsverkehr' (2010) Zeitschrift für das gesamte Schuldrecht 400.

Hartlief, Ton, 'Freedom and Protection in Contemporary Contract Law' (2004) 27 Journal of Consumer Policy 265.

Hartmut, Oetker, 'AGB-Kontrolle im Zivil- und Arbeitsrecht' (2012) 212 Archiv für die civilistische Praxis 203.

Heinrich, Christian, *Formale Freiheit und materiale Gerechtigkeit* (Mohr Siebeck 2000).

Hensen, Horst-Diether, 'Zur Entstehung des AGB-Gesetzes', in Andreas Heldrich, Peter Schlechtriem and Eike Schmidt (eds), *Recht im Spannungsfeld von Theorie und Praxis. Festschrift für Helmut Heinrichs zum 70. Geburtstag* (Beck 1998) 335.

Hesselink, Martijn W, 'SMEs in European Contract Law', in Katharina Boele-Woelki and Willem Grossheide (eds), *The Future of European Contract Law* (Wolters Kluwer 2007).

Jahn, Joachim, 'Vertragsfreiheit soll wachsen', *Frankfurter Allgemeine Zeitung* (Frankfurt 16 March 2010).

Jansen, Nils, 'Klauselkontrolle im europäischen Privatrecht' (2010) Zeitschrift für Europäisches Privatrecht 69.

Kant, Immanuel, *Metaphysik der Sitten* (vol I, Nicolovius 1797).

Kessel, Christian and Stomps, Andreas 'Haftungsklauseln im Geschäftsverkehr zwischen Unternehmern' (2009) Betriebsberater 2666.

Kessler, Friedrich, 'Contracts of Adhesion – Some Thoughts about Freedom of Contract' (1943) 43 Columbia Law Review 629.

Kieninger, Eva-Maria, 'AGB-Kontrolle von grenzüberschreitenden Geschäften im unternehmerischen Verkehr', in Peter Jung, Philipp Lamprecht, Katrin Blasek and Martin Schmidt-Kessel (eds), *Einheit und Vielheit im Unternehmensrecht. Festschrift für Uwe Blaurock zum 70. Geburtstag* (Mohr Siebeck 2013).

Koch, Robert, 'Das AGB-Recht im unternehmerischen Verkehr: Zu viel des Guten oder Bewegung in die richtige Richtung?' (2010) Betriebsberater 1811.

Kollmann, Andreas, 'AGB: Nicht nur theoretische Probleme (in) der Praxis' (2011) Neue Juristische Online-Zeitschrift 625.

Kondring, Jörg, 'Flucht vor dem deutschen AGB-Recht bei Inlandsverträgen' (2010) Recht der Internationalen Wirtschaft 184.

La Rosa, Elena, *Tecniche di regolazione del contratto e strumenti rimediali* (Giuffrè 2012).

Lando, Ole, 'Should Business Enterprises Benefit from Consumer Protection', in Günter Hager and Ingeborg Schwenzer (eds), *Festschrift für Peter Schlechtriem zum 70. Geburtstag* (Mohr Siebeck 2003).

Lando, Ole and Beale, Hugh (eds), *Principles of European Contract Law*, Parts I and II combined and revised, Prepared by the Commission on European Contract Law (Kluwer Law International 2000).

Lenkaitis, Karlheinz and Löwisch, Stephan, 'Zur Inhaltskontrolle von AGB im unternehmerischen Geschäftsverkehr' (2009) Zeitschrift für Wirtschaftsrecht 441.

Leuschner, Lars, 'AGB-Kontrolle im unternehmerischen Verkehr' (2010) Juristenzeitung 875.

Leuschner, Lars, 'Reformvorschläge für die AGB-Kontrolle im unternehmerischen Rechtsverkehr' (2015) Zeitschrift für Wirtschaftsrecht 2045.

Libertini, Mario, 'La responsabilità per abuso di dipendenza economica: la fattispecie' (2013) Contratto e impresa 1.

Libertini, Mario, 'Posizione dominante individuale e posizione dominante collettiva' (2003) Rivista di diritto commerciale I 556.

Livingston, Dorothy, 'Freedom of Contract – A Justified Override: The Business Contract Terms (Assignment of Receivables) Regulations 2018' (2019) 20 Business Law International 63.

Macario, Francesco, 'Equilibrio delle posizioni contrattuali ed autonomia privata nella subfornitura', in Lanfranco Ferroni (ed), *Equilibrio delle posizioni contrattuali ed autonomia privata* (ESI 2002).

Macario, Francesco, 'Genesi, evoluzione e consolidamento di una nuova clausola generale: il divieto di abuso di dipendenza economica' (2016) Giustizia civile 506.

Macario, Francesco, 'L'abuso dell'autonomia negoziale nei contratti tra imprenditori', in Pietro Sirena (ed), *Il diritto Europeo dei contratti d'impresa* (Giuffrè 2000).

Maier-Reimer, Georg, 'AGB-Recht im unternehmerischen Rechtsverkehr – Der BGH überdreht die Schraube' (2017) Neue Juristische Wochenschrift 1.

Mato Pacín, Mª Natalia, *Cláusulas abusivas y empresario adherente* (Agencia Estatal Boletín Oficial del Estado 2017).

Mattioni, Matteo, 'La tutela del lavoro autonomo nelle transazioni commerciali e le clausole e le condotte abusive', in Gaetano Zilio Grandi and Marco Biasi (eds), *Commentario breve allo statuto del lavoro autonomo e del lavoro agile* (Giuffré 2018).

Maugeri, Maria Rosaria, *Abuso di dipendenza economica e autonomia privata* (Giuffrè 2003).

Mengoni, Luigi, 'Forma giuridica e materia economica', in Domenico Pettiti (ed), *Studi in onore di Alberto Asquini* (vol III, Cedam 1963).

Micklitz, Hans-W, 'The Principles of European Contract Law and the Protection of the Weaker Party' (2004) 27 Journal of Consumer Policy 349.

Micklitz, Hans-W, *The Politics of Justice in European Private Law* (Cambridge University Press 2018).

Micklitz, Hans-W, 'Unfair Terms in Consumer Contracts', in Norbert Reich, Hans-W Micklitz, Peter Rott and Klaus Tonner (eds), *European Consumer Law* (2nd ed, Intersentia 2014).

Miethaner, Tobias, *AGB-Kontrolle versus Individualvereinbarung* (Mohr Siebeck 2010).

Miethaner, Tobias, 'AGB oder Individualvereinbarung – die gesetzliche Schlüsselstelle „im Einzelnen ausgehandelt"' (2010) Neue Juristische Wochenschrift 3121.

Minervini, Enrico, 'Il "terzo contratto"' (2009) I Contratti 493.

Minervini, Enrico, *L'equo compenso degli avvocati e degli altri liberi professionisti* (Giappichelli 2018).

Mogendorf, Mathias, *Der strukturell unterlegene Unternehmer* (Mohr Siebeck 2016).

Möslein, Florian, 'Die Regulierung privater Macht', in Möslein (ed), *Private Macht* (Mohr Siebeck 2016) 563.

Möslein, Florian, 'Private Macht als Forschungsgegenstand der Privatrechtswissenschaft', in Möslein (ed), *Private Macht* (Mohr Siebeck 2016) 1.

Müller, Werner, 'Die AGB-Kontrolle im unternehmerischen Geschäftsverkehr – Standortnachteil für das deutsche Recht' (2013) Betriebsberater 1355.

Müller, Werner and Schilling, Alexander, 'AGB-Kontrolle im unternehmerischen Geschäftsverkehr' (2012) Betriebsberater 2319.

Musso, Alberto, 'La subfornitura', in Antonio Scialoja and Giuseppe Branca (ed), *Commentario del codice civile* (Zanichelli 2003).

Navarretta, Emanuela, 'Principio di uguaglianza, principio di non discriminazione e contratto' (2013) Rivista di diritto civile 547.

Neuhaus, Paul H, *Die Grundbegriffe des Internationalen Privatrechts* (Mohr Siebeck 1962).

Niebling, Jürgen, 'AGB-Recht – Aktuelle Entwicklungen zu Einbeziehung, Inhaltskontrolle und Rechtsfolgen' (2014) Monatsschrift für Deutsches Recht 636.

Nuzzo, Mario, 'Condizioni generali di contratto', in Natalino Irti (ed), *Dizionario del diritto privato*, I, *Diritto Civile* (Giuffré 1980).

Osti, Cristoforo, *Nuovi obblighi a contrarre* (Giappichelli 2004).

Pagliantini, Stefano, 'Il nuovo regime della trasparenza nella direttiva sui servizi di pagamento' (2009) I contratti 1165.

Pagliantini, Stefano, 'Per una lettura dell'abuso contrattuale: contratti del consumatore, dell'imprenditore debole e della microimpresa' (2010) Rivista di diritto commerciale I 409.

Pagliantini, Stefano, 'Profili sull'integrazione del contratto abusivo parzialmente nullo', in Giovanni D'Amico and Stefano Pagliantini (eds), *Nullità per abuso ed integrazione del contratto* (Giappichelli 2013).

Pasquino, Teresa, 'D lgs 9 ottobre 2002, no 231 (come modificato dal d lgs 9 novembre 2012 no 192)', in Enrico Gabrielli (ed), *Commentario del codice civile, Delle obbligazioni* (UTET 2013).

Patti, Salvatore, 'Le condizioni generali di contratto e i contratti del consumatore', in Pietro Rescigno and Enrico Gabrielli (eds), *Trattato dei contratti, I contratti in generale* (vol I, UTET 2006).

Perulli, Adalberto, 'Il jobs act degli autonomi: nuove (e vecchie) tutele per il lavoro autonomo non imprenditoriale' (2017) Rivista italiana di diritto del lavoro 185.

Perulli, Adalberto, 'Le tutele civilistiche: il ritardo nei pagamenti; le clausole e condotte abusive', in Luigi Fiorillo and Adalberto Perulli (eds), *Il jobs act del lavoro autonomo e del lavoro agile* (Giappichelli 2018).

Pfeiffer, Thomas, 'Die Abwahl des deutschen AGB-Rechts in Inlandsfällen bei Vereinbarung eines Schiedsverfahrens' (2012) Neue Juristische Wochenschrift 1169.

Pfeiffer, Thomas, 'Flucht ins schweizerische Recht? Zu den AGB-rechtlichen Folgen der Wahl schweizerischen Rechts', in Hans Schulte-Nölke, F Christian Genzow and Barbara Grunewald (eds), *Zwischen Vertragsfreiheit und Verbraucherschutz. Festschrift für Friedrich Graf von Westphalen* (Schmidt 2010).

Pinto, Vincenzo, 'L'abuso di dipendenza economica "fuori dal contratto" tra diritto civile e diritto antitrust' (2000) Rivista di diritto civile 400.

Plato, 'Protagoras or the Sophists', in *Plato in Twelve Volumes* (vol 3, Walter R.M. Lamb tr, Harvard University Press/William Heinemann Ltd 1967).

Prosperi, Francesco, *Il contratto di subfornitura e l'abuso di dipendenza economica* (ESI 2002).

Raiser, Ludwig, *Das Recht der Allgemeinen Geschäftsbedingungen* (Hanseatische Verlagsanstalt 1935).

Raiser, Ludwig, 'Vertragsfreiheit heute' (1958) Juristenzeitung 1.

Raiser, Ludwig, 'Vertragsfunktion und Vertragsfreiheit', in Ernst von Caemmerer et al. (eds), *100 Jahre Deutsches Rechtsleben   Festschrift zum hundertjähi igen Bestehen des Deutschen Juristentags 1960–1960* (Müller 1960).

Rakoff, Todd D, 'The Law and Sociology of Boilerplate', in Omri Ben-Shahar (ed), *Boilerplate. The Foundation of Market Contracts* (Cambridge University Press 2007).

Raz, Joseph, *Between Authority and Interpretation: On the Theory of Law and Practical Reason* (Oxford University Press 2009).

Renna, Luca, 'L'abuso di dipendenza economica come fattispecie transtipica' (2013) Contratto e impresa 375.

Rescigno, Pietro, 'Premessa', in *Trattato di diritto dei contratti*, vol I, *I contratti in generale* (UTET 2006).

Reuter, Dieter, 'Die etischen Grundlagen des Privatrechts – formale Freiheitsethik oder materiale Verantwortungsethik?' (1989) 189 Archiv für die civilistische Praxis 199.

Romano, Valerio Cosimo, 'Problemi scelti in tema di abuso di dipendenza economica da ritardo nei pagamenti commerciali' (2017) Danno e responsabilità 380.

Roppo, Vincenzo, 'Contratto di diritto comune, contratto del consumatore, contratto con asimmetria di potere contrattuale: genesi e sviluppi' (2001) Rivista di diritto privato 769.

Roppo, Vincenzo, 'Dal contratto del consumatore al contratto asimmetrico (schivando il 'terzo contratto')?' in Giuseppe Vettori (ed), *Remedies in Contract* (Cedam 2008).

Roppo, Vincenzo, 'From Consumer Contracts to Asymmetric Contracts: a Trend in European Contract Law' (2009) European Review of Contract Law 304.

Roppo, Vincenzo, 'Parte generale del contratto, contratti del consumatore e contratti asimmetrici (con postilla sul "terzo contratto")' (2007) Rivista di diritto privato 679.

Rott, Peter, 'Unfair Contract Terms', in Christian Twigg-Flessner (ed), *Research Handbook on EU Consumer Law and Contract Law* (Edward Elgar 2016).

Rühl, Giesela, 'The Battle of the Forms: Comparative and Economic Observations' (2003) 24 University of Pennsylvania Journal of International Economic Law 189.

Rummel, Peter, '§ 864a', in Peter Rummel and Lukas Meinhard (eds), *ABGB Kommentar zum Allgemeinen Bürgerlichen Gesetzbuch* (Manz 2015).

Russo, Ennio, 'Imprenditore Debole, Imprenditore-Persona, Abuso di Dipendenza Economica, 'Terzo Contratto'' (2009) Contratto e impresa 120.

Sacco, Rodolfo and De Nova, Giorgio, 'Obbligazioni e contratti', in Pietro Rescigno (ed), *Trattato di diritto privato* (Utet 1999).

Schiller, Michael, 'Inequality of Bargaining Power versus Market for Lemons: Legal Paradigm Change and the Court of Justice's Jurisprudence on Directive 93/13 on Unfair Contract Terms' (2008) 33 ELRev 336.

Schlosser, Peter F, '§ 310', in Michael Martinek (ed), *J von Staudingers Kommentar zum BGB, Buch 2* (Sellier - de Gruyter 2013).

Schulte-Nölke, Hans, '"No Market for 'Lemons"': On the Reasons for a Judicial Unfairness Test for B2B Contracts' (2015) European Review of Private Law 195.

Schwartz, Alan and Scott, Robert, 'Contracts theory and the limits of contract law' (2003) 113 YaleLJ 541.

Schweitzer, Heike, 'Wettbewerbsrecht und das Problem privater Macht', in Florian Möslein (ed), *Private Macht* (Mohr Siebeck 2016) 449.

Schwenzer, Ingeborg and Marti Whitebread, Claudio, 'International B2B Contracts – Freedom Unchained?' (2015) 4 Penn St J L & Int'l Aff 43.

Scognamiglio, Renato, 'Dei contratti in generale', in Antonio Scialoja and Giuseppe Branca (eds), *Commentario del codice civile* (Zanichelli 1992).

Scognamiglio, Renato, 'Statuti dell'autonomia privata e regole ermeneutiche nella prospettiva storica e nella contrapposizione tra parte generale e disciplina di settore' (2005) Europa e diritto privato 1015.

Spolidoro, Marco Saverio, 'Riflessioni critiche sul rapporto tra abuso di posizione dominante e abuso dell'altrui dipendenza economica' (1999) Rivista di diritto industriale I 195.

Stöhr, Alexander, *Kleine Unternehmen* (Mohr Siebeck 2019).

Stuyck, Jules, 'Do We Need 'Consumer Protection' for Small Businesses at the EU Level?', in Kai Purnhagen and Peter Rott (eds), *Varieties of European Economic Law and Regulation* (Springer 2014).

Twigg-Flesner, Christian, 'The EU's Proposals for Regulating B2B Relationships on Online Platforms – Transparency, Fairness and Beyond' (2018) EuCML 222.

Twigg-Flesner, Christian, *Europeanisation of Contract Law* (2nd ed, Routledge 2013).

Valentino, Daniela, 'Timeo Danaos et dona ferentes. La tutela del consumatore e delle microimprese nelle pratiche commerciali scorrette' (2013) Rivista di diritto civile 1157.

von Hippel, Eike, *Der Schutz des Schwächeren* (Mohr Siebeck 1982).

Wieacker, Franz, *Das Sozialmodell der klassischen Privatrechtsgesetzbücher und die Entwicklung der modernen Gesellschaft* (Müller 1953).

Wieacker, Franz, *Privatrechtsgeschichte der Neuzeit unter besonderer Berücksichtigung der deutschen Entwicklung* (Vandenhoeck und Ruprecht 1967).

Wilhelmsson, Thomas, 'Various Approaches to Unfair Terms and Their Background Philosophies' (2008) XIV Juridica International 51.

Wurmnest, Wolfgang, '§ 307', '§ 308', '§ 309', in Franz Jürgen Säcker, Roland Rixecker, Hartmut Oetker and Bettina Limperg (eds), *Münchener Kommentar zum BGB* (Beck 2019).

Zaccaria, Alessio, 'art 1341', 'art 1342' and 'art 1370', in Giorgio Cian and Alberto Trabucchi (eds), *Commentario breve al codice civile* (Wolters Kluver/Cedam, 2018).

Zoppini, Andrea, 'Il contratto asimmetrico tra parte generale, contratti di impresa e disciplina della concorrenza' (2008) Rivista di diritto civile I 536.

Index